"Wow, this book was refreshing, empowering, enlightening, and encouraging. Carly Spina has written a book to equip a select group of teachers to reach a unique group of learners and she has left me with new tools, strategies, and mindsets to reach virtually any learner I am blessed to teach. Thank you, Carly for reminding us all that respect is given, not earned and that it is up to us to show that respect to all of those that we serve, both young and old."

— **DR. DAVE SCHMITTOU**, DIRECTOR OF
LEADERSHIP & DEVELOPMENT, TEACH
BETTER TEAM

"*Moving Beyond for Multilingual Learners* is a book that I have been waiting to be written! Carly Spina has so much knowledge, experience and her ideas have already changed my thinking and approach when supporting our multilingual learners. You're going to love the stories from Carly, you're going to use the strategies from Carly, and you're going to recommend this book to your colleagues so they can do the same!"

— **ADAM WELCOME**, PRINCIPAL, AUTHOR,
SPEAKER, PODCASTER

"In *Moving Beyond*, Spina brings an INSPIRING strengths-based approach filled with culturally responsive best practices to educators' work with multilingual learners. Spina writes with the heartwarming passion and CREDIBILITY of an award winning change agent fueled to reimagine school for all students. This book is BURSTING with practical strategies, kid-tested ideas, and intentional solutions from powerful pedagogy that delivers on the hope of reaching societal impact. Simply put, this is a must have resource! *Moving Beyond* has my HIGHEST recommendation possible!"

— **HANS APPEL**, EDUCATOR, WRITER, SPEAKER AND AUTHOR OF *AWARD WINNING CULTURE: BUILDING WHOLE-CHILD INTENTIONALITY AND ACTION THROUGH CHARACTER, EXCELLENCE, AND COMMUNITY*

"*Moving Beyond* is a powerful resource for any educator serving culturally and linguistically diverse students. It is a great combination of inspiration and practical ideas. Not only does Spina give examples of how we can best advocate and support our students and their families, she shares her ideas with humor, vulnerability and a strong message of respect for the diverse families we serve."

— **CAROL SALVA**, EDUCATOR, SPEAKER, CO-AUTHOR OF *BOOSTING ACHIEVEMENT: REACHING STUDENTS WITH INTERRUPTED OR MINIMAL EDUCATION* AND CO-AUTHOR OF *DIY PD FOR TEACHERS OF MULTILINGUAL LEARNERS*

"Carly Spina is able to establish a relationship with the reader through in-depth stories and real world examples from over 15 years in education. Her passion for supporting educators to provide the best instructional support to all students is evident on every page of this book. This is a must read for all educators because all students are language learners."

— **JEANETTE SIMENSON-GUROLNICK**, EDUCATOR, SPEAKER, DIRECTOR OF PROGRAMMING, THRIVELY

MOVING BEYOND FOR MULTILINGUAL LEARNERS

INNOVATIVE SUPPORTS FOR LINGUISTICALLY DIVERSE STUDENTS

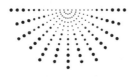

CARLY SPINA

EduMatch PUBLISHING

CONTENTS

DEDICATION

To my husband Eric-
Thank you for always encouraging me and supporting me. You are
forever my best friend and I love you so much.

To TJ & Chloe-
You two are my whole world and I love you more than words can
say. Always believe in yourself and in others, and dream big. God's
got you.

To Ashley, Danielle, Momma, & Daddy-
You made me who I am today. Thank you for always being my safe
space and my soft landing.

To my friends, family, and my PLN-
Thank you for supporting me & helping me grow!

BEYOND YOUR TITLE

EMBRACING YOUR SPACE AS A CHANGE AGENT

ow, am I glad to see you! I've been waiting for a leader like you. Ready to start a fire? Ready to advocate? Those we serve need us. We need each other. Let's go.

I started writing because I want to light you up. I want to reignite the fire in your heart that serves our amazing multilingual students, families, and communities. I need other fire starters. This is why I'm so glad you picked this up. Imagine how we can light things up when we serve together with blazing passion in our hearts.

This isn't a research book. There's a ton of great research books out there, and if you're looking for those, please reach out—I have great recommendations and a long list of favorite researchers! This is a collection of stories, thoughts, ideas, questions, and most of all —hope & encouragement. Research is needed—because we must be grounded in best practice, but our hope is also needed—it's the water that keeps us going. We need a steady diet of both.

I want this book to help us look beyond "achievement gaps" and the "just add visuals" approach to really creating powerful opportunities for all students, including (and especially) our multilingual learners.

This journey is **ours** that we can write and rewrite together! We are going to share some ideas, thoughts, and challenges. I'm going to share pieces of my blog, *Moving Beyond for Multilingual Learners*, throughout the book. I'll share my personal stories, my professional stories, and my mistakes throughout this book. We may giggle together. We may mess up some things and flop some ideas together. Yes, we are going to cry a little bit, too. Advocacy is hard work. However, we are going to overcome a lot together. I'm a big virtual high-fiver. If there was a High-Five Gif available, I'd put one right here (and maybe a virtual hug, too).

The truth is we need each other. Teaching is hard. Leading is difficult. Being a change agent is challenging. We have to surround ourselves with positive supports, a strong network, and a wide net that can lift us up because we are undoubtedly going to get pushback. If we need to take breaks, let's take breaks. If we need to unplug for a bit, that's okay, too. We just can't give up.

We do so much more than just teach. All educators do—it's true. None of us is "just a teacher." I feel like that phrase—just a teacher—is one that should just not exist in any language. None of us simply teach—*we serve*. Additionally, we don't only serve our learners—we serve students, families, colleagues, our schools, our districts, and our communities. We have a huge responsibility on our shoulders—no wonder we are so tired all the time!

The role of educators serving multilingual students was never a role that was only about acquiring a language. While roles may look different in each setting, the folks serving have the same passion and fire to lead beyond their title. It's truly the role of a change agent.

Today's educators who are serving multilingual students are educators full of fire. There's a passion to educate, inspire, and empower students by expanding their linguistic assets. There's a passion to connect, support, and empower families by ensuring they have what they need and amplifying their voices. There's a passion to educate, push, challenge, and empower colleagues to make decisions with our students at the forefront. Our job keeps students at the center of our work, but it expands to a larger sphere of influence that we can impact.

YOU ARE A GIFT TO OUR FIELD!

You are uniquely you. Your experiences have shaped you into the person you are today. You've survived your hardships, you've won personal battles within your heart and mind, and you have experienced challenges in your personal and professional life. These experiences make up how you live and lead—the good, the bad, the high, and the low. You've learned lessons and gained wisdom through them. They are a part of your story. Don't let folks dismiss you because of the number of years you've served in a classroom.

You have passions that are unique to you. You may be a gardener, dancer, coder, baker, or designer. You have passions that light you up. You have things that make your heart happy—that either help you unwind, or wind you up! These are also a part of your story.

There are talents that you hold that are unlike others'. You may be a great listener, or you may be exceptionally organized. You may have the ability to get anyone in the room to laugh. You may have the ability to know just the right words to say to a student who's struggling. You may be a talented speaker, artist, or fitness coach. Your talents are a part of your story.

You hold unique experiences that have shaped the person you are today. You have overcome obstacles, walked through storms, accomplished goals, failed, and succeeded. You have walked your own journey in your lifetime thus far that no one else has. Your experiences have brought you to this very moment.

All these beautiful components make up the person you are. Tap into them. Recognize them. Invite them more into your heart, your conversations, your classroom, your school.

You are a special human being, indeed. There is no one else like you. You have things to say, gifts to share, and experiences that will help you lead. Own all the parts of you and use them to lead for the needed change.

Step into your space as a change agent and leader. No matter what your title is, how many years of professional experience you have under your belt, or how many nay-sayers you have in your environment… you are still a leader for change.

KNOWING OUR OWN STORIES

Each of us has stories and experiences that have shaped our lives.

Lincoln Square in the 80s and 90s was awesome. People were outside every day and neighbors truly looked out for each other. It was also a turbulent time for local gangs to obtain control of the area. There were several rivals, but there was a mutual understanding that the gangs were careful—looking out for the kids in the neighborhood. Whenever there was an anticipated bout of trouble, the younger siblings of the gangs would ride around on their bikes and tell the kids of the neighborhood to be inside by 8 pm or to avoid the park down the block.

While my sisters and I attended school, the teachers would teach us to "stay the path" and to avoid gangs. I believe one of my sister's 8th-grade field trips was to jail or juvenile detention center to "scare everyone straight." My mom was a youth pastor at a church in our neighborhood. She would become infuriated after talks we'd receive from teachers or pastors about how "bad" the kids in gangs were.

I remember one day very clearly when I was sharing my day with my mom. I told her about how a teacher said that gangs were for losers and none of us kids in class should end up like that. She paused and asked me what I thought. I told her that I didn't have a desire to join a gang and neither did any of my friends. She then sat down next to me at the table and said very quietly, "Gangs are not for losers. Why do you think kids are joining gangs in the first place?" I told her I didn't know.

She told me that there's no such thing as a bad kid. She said that kids join gangs for lots of reasons, many of which we may never understand. Many kids need something to belong to, and many want or need to feel safe or protected. She said that just because I had the privilege of feeling a part of something doesn't give me or anyone else the right to criticize someone else's reasons for joining a gang. It's a conversation that has stuck with me.

My mom took me to bookstores all the time. One of our favorites was called Women and Children First in Andersonville in Chicago. We'd spend hours pouring through books. She introduced me to Maya Angelou, Phyllis Wheatley, Coretta Scott King. She brought me and my sisters to the library on Lincoln Avenue where we checked out books about Cesar Chavez and Nelson Mandela. She took us to the movies to see Malcolm X in 1992 and Selena in 1997. For every white "hero" we were asked to study in school, she had 4 additional heroes for us to learn about. When we'd go to the toy store, she'd ask us to count the Barbies. How many were white? How many weren't? Why are there so many white dolls? Why aren't there the same amount with other skin colors? While my classmates were writing book reports about Goosebumps, we were reading Amos Fortune. I think my sister's 7th-grade teacher even told my mom at one point, "It's okay for the girls to read other things, too." My mom laughed because we read lots of those things too, but for reports—she wanted us to write about people who mattered.

My mom pushed us to question everything. She made us aware of our white skin and talked to us about race, religion, privilege, and socioeconomic status. We volunteered in soup kitchens as kids. She taught us to find out what our passions were, what our talents were—and use our skills to serve others.

When we were young, my dad put himself to work building porches and decks for people in the neighborhood. He started his own auto glass company, which still stands today. He didn't let anyone shame him for not going to college. He taught us to push yourself until you're proud. He taught his three girls to look out for ourselves, look out for each other, and look out for others. When business was good, he'd treat all the neighborhood kids to ice cream from the ice cream truck.

When we moved to the suburbs, I struggled. My sister and I were being given a tour by one of the guidance counselors for folks who were new to the area. We were enthralled with how large the school was. We were mesmerized by the computer lab full of computers. We were shocked at entire hallways dedicated to science labs. We were impressed by the school's carpeted hallways and the fact that they had swimming pools. When the guidance counselor told us that the school had heat and air-conditioning, he gave us quizzical looks as we high-fived each other.

We discovered within the first few days of school that we were not on the same page as most kids in our school. We learned quickly that while there was some diversity, it wasn't anything like it was when we lived in the city. We got into arguments with people constantly. We didn't understand the classmates that we had to sit next to in classes who often demonstrated a lack of empathy and seemed clueless about the world and yet they seemed to have traveled all over it. Kids left messes all over the cafeteria and said that someone else would clean it up. I once had a girl who point-blank asked me why I was wearing what I had on and why my clothes were so baggy. I stared at my clothes and I stared at hers. I didn't even know how to reply without yelling.

I failed a few classes during my freshman year, which shocked my family because I always knew how to play the game of school very well. I learned that it was very easy to "slip through the cracks" academically, so I let myself. I was depressed. I didn't like where we were. I missed my friends in the city. I missed my neighborhood and my life. I missed the sounds and sights of my block and the people who lived on it. I missed the summer nights of collecting bugs and making up dances under streetlights with my best friends.

While depressed, I also felt extremely guilty. My dad worked hard for us to move to the suburbs, and all I wanted was to go back to the city.

I had labeled almost everyone in high school as "preppy." I hated the brand names they wore, and I despised the music they listened to. I loathed that they all had grown up with professionally manicured lawns and that the student parking lot was full of BMWs and Range Rovers. The privilege was up to my ears. I started to connect with some kids who I thought were "real," and most of them were from other towns—some were even from the city, like me.

I didn't give half the kids a chance based on what they wore and how rich I assumed they were. I judged everyone and I knew they were judging me, too.

I had an urban studies class during my second or third year of high school. I was so excited to take a class where I'd finally feel like I knew something—as I could finally be the expert. At 16, I was pretty convinced that with my upbringing, I *knew* Chicago and I could teach these suburbanites a thing or two.

One day the teacher asked everyone a question about the alleys. The class was silent, even the boys who almost always spoke even when they didn't have anything to say. To prompt us further, the teacher asked us, "Well, who hung out in the alleys?" My hand shot up in the air. *Yes!* I knew that answer and I was proud to have the only hand up. The teacher called on me and I announced rather confidently: "the gangs." It was like one of those moments in a movie where the music stops playing and everyone turns to hear who just farted. I felt like every eye in the room was on me for two solid minutes of silence before the teacher said, "Umm… no…. Horses. The alleys were for horses." I know my face was bright red. Still, it was a neat class and I ended up learning a ton.

High school got better as the years went on and I found my group of friends and eventually fell in love with cheerleading (how's that for preppy, huh?). It took me up to my 4th year to finally feel somewhat connected.

When it was time for college, I knew I needed to be back in the city, so we packed up my yellow Beetle and I moved into the dorms of North Park University in the Albany Park area. I met amazing people who are still my best friends today. I was excited to be a college cheerleader and I joined the Latin American Student Association (LASO). It was run by my best friends and roommates Zully, Christina, and Karina.

I always wanted to be a teacher. I've always loved kids. While I was in college, I dove right into my education courses eager to learn everything so I could be the best teacher I could be. Through my various experiences in schools as a preservice teacher, I saw inequities firsthand. As education students, we worked in Chicago Public Schools, private schools, and I even ended up doing my student-teaching in my high school's neighborhood (yes, out in the suburbs). I saw what the schools had in terms of resources. I saw how kids were treated differently. I also saw how dismissive many people were of the inequities—especially people of privilege. It struck a nerve.

THE WHY

Knowing that we are in this for the long haul, we have to stay centered in our Why, and I want us to be careful in our Why question. It's not about remembering why you became a teacher. Many of us had lots of different reasons and visions for what we wanted to do in our careers when we first started, but for some of us, those reasons may change over the years as we grow in our passions, our talents, our experiences, and our leadership. The question then becomes: Why do you do what you do each day?

For me, my personal Why has grown a lot over the years. I used to say that I wanted to make a difference. It felt good to say that out loud—it felt very noble. However, I didn't lay out exactly how I wanted to make a difference. Today, my Why looks different.

I took my first job out of college as a 20-year old with a suburban public school district as an EL teacher for 3rd, 4th, and 5th grade. After feeling pretty confident, I bombed the interview with over 15 people around the table, and I got the phone call that they wanted to hire me. Off I went.

My first classroom was in a mobile unit. I had no idea the amount of state paperwork that needed to be complete before beginning EL services. I was anxious to start seeing kids, and I couldn't wait to receive my formal training to administer our language screeners so I could spend time with the kids. I was ready to teach!

I stumbled, learned, messed up, bombed observations,

improved, asked for advice, and sought feedback. They were a messy few years of growth. Then, the EL team at work started to expand and I felt like we could do some pretty big things for kids. I served the school for five years as an EL teacher and then applied for a third-grade classroom position in our Transitional Bilingual Program (English/Spanish). I was psyched when I got the position. Through my six years in that role, I learned so much from my kids and my families—far more than I feel like I ever taught them.

I later served as a district-wide Multilingual Instructional Coach. The programs grew larger, boasting over 65 languages across the district.

Over the years, yes—my Why has changed and developed right along with me. What's my Why today?

Lenses need to be flipped. Paradigms need to be shifted. I want people to put our kids front and center, elevate them, and bring their talents and passions into the classroom. I want teachers to feel empowered in their instruction, knowing that they have just the right tools to reach and teach everyone. I want all families to feel like an integral part of the school and school community. I want our administrators to lead with equity not just in mind, but at the forefront of what they do.

From the Blog: Spheres of Influence

Have you ever said to someone that you are not a decision-maker?

I have. I have said. this. out. loud. Not just once, but on multiple occasions.

Ugh.

By simply thinking in this way, I have limited my impact. By saying it aloud, I have limited my ability to influence change. I have abdicated responsibility. I have removed myself from the equation completely.

I have silenced my voice *just by simply thinking* it. I have a constant yearning to amplify my voice, but I degrade myself over and over when I've said that I have no decision-making ability.

Walking into a space declaring that you cannot make decisions demonstrates a fixed mindset, and that's been a rough realization for me, but it's one that I need to tackle. I often tell other educators that we are not JUST educators—we are the front lines for our kids, we are the advocates, the change agents, and the difference makers.

The same goes for me. I'm not here to sit back and be complacent. I'm not here to feel sorry for myself and wish that I could change things. I'm not here to sit quietly at meetings to the point of frustration.

I'm a change agent. I'm someone who's going to ask the challenging questions. I'm someone who's going to make a difference for kids, families, teachers, and communities. I'm going to lead, inspire, and flip lenses.

I'm also going to fail. A lot. I'm going to cry into my pillow some nights. I'm going to have pauses, bumps, & bruises. I'm going to have to revisit a few things over and over again. I will have to fail forward. I will mess up, ask for forgiveness, and grow.

But I'm not going to stop.

On those moments where I'm feeling stuck, I'm going to reframe my thinking. I'm going to recognize that I (like you!) have several spheres of influence. I can use my spheres to initiate change, push thinking, and support my teammates & colleagues. I can utilize my spheres to participate in discussions, collect feedback, & get a different perspective. I can engage my spheres of influence to ask the difficult questions with me.

I have to start by identifying my circles that I am a part of both personally and professionally. I can think of my teams in each building I serve, each school I serve, each committee I'm a part of, and my social groups to which I belong. I can consider my online networks (Facebook groups, Twitter PLN, and Instagram friends). I can reflect on my group of close girlfriends and their families. I think of my neighbors, those I volunteer with, and colleagues that I used to work with years ago.

Ummm...Wow. That's a lot of folks, and I haven't even scratched the surface.

Seriously, go grab a pen right now and do this. Write them all out. It's going to kind of blow your mind a little bit.

I have a HUGE ABILITY to make an impact. SO
DO YOU.

I can shake things up, ruffle feathers, and do some major disrupting! SO CAN YOU.

How would you define your current role? Perhaps your title is that of a teacher, a principal, a coach, or a consultant. Beyond your title, I want you to think about what your role entails. Who do you serve?

Have you ever heard of imposter syndrome? Many describe it as a lack of confidence, that feeling that you don't quite have what it takes yet to do the work that you are being asked to do. Even though you are very qualified to do the work, you doubt yourself and your abilities. Many will also tell you that this affects more women than men, and more people of color than Caucasian. We are told, "Fake it 'till you make it." Simply act like you know what you're doing until you know what you're doing. No matter how many years of experience you may have, it can be easy to second-guess our skills, talents, and leadership. However, we need to become aware of our thinking so that we can correct it the moment those thoughts creep in.

I was a teacher for 11 years. In those years, I served many—but I had this erroneous assumption that I could serve *more* if I was in a different role. *I was wrong.* If you are a teacher, I want you to reflect on this a bit. Make a list of all those you serve on a daily or weekly basis. These may include:

- your students
- your students' parents and guardians
- your teammates and colleagues
- your school
- your community

Outside of these, you may also belong to school-level or district-level committees. You may belong to professional organizations or an active PLN (professional learning network) online. If you wrote out your list as described in the blog activity, take a look at it—you may even marvel at how long this list is! You are making a deep impact on all of those you serve. This is an extraordinary task. You are charged with deeply affecting all of these people—wow!

Now think again of that ripple effect. *Woah.* As an educator, you have the extraordinary ability and platform to serve others in a way that's never been done before. You have the scope to change systems, disrupt the status quo, flip lenses, and push on issues. This is huge.

For whatever your role is, I want you to look at that list of all of those folks you are serving, and then go that extra step to consider your ripple effect. Consider these spheres of influence that you can impact. What circles, teams, or networks are they a part of?

For whatever reason you picked up this book, I want you to pause and consider this moment. I want you to take this in right now. YOU ARE A CHANGE AGENT. You are a leader. You have the power to effect change. That is power, indeed. Step into this space that you have been called. Own it. Hold it tightly with both hands. It's yours.

You must *feel empowered* to empower those around you. Being empowered doesn't necessarily mean you hold decision-making power in your school, district, or system. Being empowered means owning your skills, talents, and experiences and using them to lift others. You can do this in so many ways.

Leadership transcends titles.

STEPPING INTO OUR SPACES

In our roles, we have an opportunity to serve in big ways—but we have to fully step into our roles and own the full scope of them. We have to firmly plant our feet into these shoes by recognizing the opportunity we have to serve. We have to lace up these shoes by acknowledging that this is going to be a long run. I hate running, so I find it quite ironic that I'm using a running metaphor here, but we have to remember—the scope of being an agent for change is not for short stints of time here and there. It's like the saying goes—this is a marathon, not a sprint.

There will be days where our shoes give us blisters. There will be days where we cannot run, so we have to walk instead. There will be days where we just stand in place, but we're still standing in those shoes. Some days bring us to our knees, and we try desperately to keep moving forward. We are so fatigued, beat down, and overwhelmed sometimes that we just collapse entirely. But even while we lie face down on the floor, out of breath, out of energy, out of will… we still have the shoes on our feet. The shoes themselves may fall apart. They may require some ingenuity and some duct tape to stay on sometimes. Sometimes they may carry us to new places.

We live in a time where equity, in some settings, has become nothing more than a buzzword, and the people who often preach it the loudest don't understand what it means. We live in a time where we talk about inclusion as an ideal but we lack the structures and the mindsets to truly embrace it. We live in a time where our culturally and linguistically diverse students are left out of the equation.

You may say to me,—*Gee Carly, I see what you're saying, but I actually don't have a high number of language learners in my classroom, or even in my school. I can't relate!*—I hear ya, friend, but let me break this down for you. Your school is full of students. Your community is full of families. In every school, school district, and community, I will tell you this (and this is so unfortunate, but so true): there are student and family populations who need additional support **and** there are entire groups who have been historically underserved. They may have been marginalized by our school systems and our society in some way, shape, or form: their sexual orientation (or that of their family members), their faith, their socioeconomic status, or even what part of town in which they live. This book is for all educators, serving all children. Unfortunately, our society has a long history of creating "others" who fall outside of norms. We have "otherized" large numbers of students and parents. This work is surely for you, too.

The purpose of this book is to light you up. I hope to equip you with some powerful tools for your teacher-leader toolkit, pose some challenging questions for you to consider and reconsider, and help you grow in your ability to serve and advocate. As we travel this road together, you will have your eyes opened to all the possibilities that begin with the question, "Is this benefitting *all* students, or is it just benefiting a majority of students?" We are living and functioning in education systems that were designed for a majority—so one group of learners from the majority is benefitting, but what happens to those outside of the majority?

THE "REAL" (AND SCARY) WORLD

There is a lot out there that we must grapple with and form our own opinions about—hate crimes, immigration policy, anti-immigrant rhetoric, child detention centers, etc. These topics are real. We live in a world that is full of race tensions, linguistic oppression, and marginalizations of people. Regardless of our political affiliations, we are advocates for *all* children—no matter what.

Our students are feeling these pressures and are burdened with their weight. They overhear their neighbors talking. They watch their parents coping with these stressors. They hear snippets on the news. Some have had these experiences touch their families. They are carrying so much, whether we know it or not.

While we cannot take away all of our students' stressors, we can create learning environments that are safe and welcoming. We can remain steadfast in our resolve to get our students and families what they need. We can fight for them behind closed doors. We can stand alongside families at the PTA meetings and Board of Education meetings. We can support the structures that seek to amplify their voices instead of having folks speak for them.

It is on us, *now more than ever*, to ensure that our students and families feel that school is a place in which they belong.

VOCAB LESSON: WHAT ARE WE TALKING ABOUT HERE?

Let's start with some clarity on terminology, shall we? As an educator of language acquisition, I know that it's important to build some understanding of the vocabulary words that we'll use frequently throughout this journey. Let's start with the best part of our job—our students.

In this book, I will be using the collective "we." We seem to fall into traps when we assign students with labels: Gifted, At-Risk, English Learners (or ELs), IEP students, etc. We even take this a step further sometimes by assigning our students additional and more judgemental layers of labels: troubled, low, behavior kids, disconnected, unmotivated, lost kids, kids who don't care... or even my personal favorite—"relationship kids." You know, those kids who do better and have more success if they have a supportive and caring relationship with their teacher. Why do people use this phrase as if this is only limited to certain students? Aren't *all* kids "relationship kids?" Aren't *all* humans relational beings? But I digress.

There's no such thing as a "low kid." There's just not. There are plenty of kids who have been underserved, undersupported, or not given the same opportunity. There is plenty of research to support this. Students who have been marginalized by society are not expected to accomplish the same things as their Caucasian, monolingual counterparts, or their peers who have socioeconomic privilege. Instead of administrative teams who identify this opportunity gap, they instead place the fault on the student, declaring them a "low kid."

No student is low. Chances are if they are underperforming on a random assessment, they may have been held to lower standards because of their last name, skin color, or the language spoken at home. It is also quite possible that the assessment itself presents a type of bias and may not be the best indicator of what that student is capable of and/or it does not accurately demonstrate their ability nor potential.

Let's consider the word choices we use in terms of who our language learners are. After 15 years of working with language acquisition education, I've heard my fair share, and perhaps you have, too. In 2006, Illinois defined students as being "NEPs," or "Non-English Proficient." Wow. What's the first word you see? "Non." As in, NOT. That's the FIRST word we chose to use when describing this student population. We have defined students by what they cannot do. How empowering, right? I'd insert a big eye-roll GIF here if I could. But alas, we moved on as a state. We decided to change things up and cut our kids a break and instead used the term "LEP," or Limited English Proficient. Again, let's define kids by their limitations. Are we serious? In much of our state reporting systems, we still are being asked to use this demeaning label. Ugh. Most recently, the state of Illinois (inspired by the WIDA Consortium) has embraced the term Multilingual Learner.

I've also heard lots of other words to describe our students:

- ELL- English Language Learners
- ESL- English as a Second Language (what if they have more than 2 languages?)
- EL- English Learners
- CLD- Culturally and Linguistically Diverse
- ML- Multilingual Learners
- EBs- Emergent Bilinguals
- DLs- Dual Learners (or those who are being served in a dual-language program)
- SLIFE- Students with Limited or Interrupted Formal Education

I'm sure I could go on and on with this list. What do you notice about these terms and others that you have heard? What words have you found that feels best to you and why? What words would you want your children to be described as if your child was assigned a label?

Most folks will agree that the way we talk *to* kids matters. Let's move beyond that statement. The way we talk *about* kids matters, too. The way we talk about our students reflects our mindsets and beliefs about them.

I was at a conference a few years ago in Madison, Wisconsin. We had a great dialogue about this very topic. One educator pushed my thinking and asked why we have to assign everything an acronym? We all laughed because we all know how true this is —it seems like everything in education gets an acronym. She then asked if anyone's school district assigns the kids in their gifted/advanced/accelerated programs an acronym? No one had a school district that did this. We reflected for a few minutes together about why this is. We thought about how programs like these seem elevated in everyone's mind. Many districts state the full title of the program—kids, teachers, parents, administrators. Interesting, right?

This has me thinking. What if we assigned a gifted label to our linguistically diverse students? What if we called our students "Linguistically Advanced," "Linguistically Accelerated," "Linguistically Gifted," or "Linguistically Talented?" You see where I'm going with this, right? Why do some student groups have the prestige of having their full program named in totality in conversations, forms, and documents, and all "others" are reduced to a few letters?

Our kids' languages are a gift, a blessing, a SKILL, a talent! Why can't we name them by their assets? The title of our programs and the way we identify our students speaks volumes to how we view them. Hopefully, we can all consider an asset-based lens of what our kids can do and not by what they haven't yet mastered.

I would have a long name if I was constantly defined by my place of work by all the things I can't do yet: Non-Snapchat-Proficient, Non-Certified-to-Teach-Chemistry, Limited Understanding of Excel Spreadsheets, Non-French-Speaker, Limited-Proficiency-of-Pre-Calculus. Yikes. That doesn't make me look so good, does it? What if I had to introduce myself as all of these things when I met new teammates, or colleagues on Twitter, or my heroes at conferences?

We introduce our students in much the same way when we pass on student files or notes to the next teacher or school that has the privilege of serving our wonderful kids. Y'all. Our language choices matter. They matter SO. MUCH.

What if we dropped labels altogether and just called students, "students?"

We even do this weird thing where we assign responsibility: when we use phrases like "those kids" or even "the kids in that program," this is a deliberate declaration of abdicating the responsibility for their success. Students should never be "those kids," rather, *our kids*. This is such a simple language difference, but the sentiment changes completely. *All kids are our kids.*

One particular phrase that makes me itchy is when we call students *at-risk*. We make this declaration about *entire student groups*. As if, on the whole, they are at-risk of failing because of something they are doing or not doing, something they have or don't have, and the responsibility is theirs alone. What if we intentionally flipped that language? Are the students at-risk, *or are WE at-risk of not filling their needs as a school system?* Maybe we should put ourselves on the intervention list. Furthermore, it is entirely problematic when we make declarations that all multilingual learners are at-risk. Each student is unique, and as we will discuss later, multilingual learners are not a homogenous group.

We need to stop assuming that all multilingual learners are "at-risk." We need to stop assuming that students who are under a certain income threshold come from chaos. We need to drop judgments that we make about families we serve. We need to start getting serious and reflect on our personal beliefs demonstrated through our language choices that put our biases in the spotlight.

To take this a step further, I want you to consider how your phrasing is set up in your settings. Consider your data meetings, problem-solving meetings, Multi-Tiered Systems of Supports (MTSS) meetings, etc. There's always a part of each team gathering where we identify meeting norms. Typically, these norms fall somewhere along the lines of "Let's honor our time together by starting and ending on time" and "Let's identify a note taker for today and review our talking points at the end of the meeting."

What if we also took the time to identify language norms before digging into data?

I have tried this strategy of Identifying Language Norms in meetings I've attended. It has felt uncomfortable at times but has also been well-received at other times. I start by laying out common words and phrases that may have been said in prior meetings or other learning spaces. To be a little less threatening, it may be helpful to add that you've heard these phrases in other schools or districts you've served or supported so that no one feels that they're being called out. I display deficit-based phrases with a line through them so that educators and leaders around the table can see that this is no longer an acceptable phrase. I also provide an alternative phrase to use in its place. For example, see these options below:

~~They're low in both languages.~~	They are developing in both languages.
~~They can't...~~	They can...
~~They're not motivated.~~	They're not motivated by _____
~~They're low.~~	They're growing and need more support in...
~~They have limited English.~~	They're developing English skills.

By getting specific about the language that we are using and the language that imposes a deficit-lens mindset, we can collectively move towards a more asset-based lens in our school community. If we can check our language choices at the forefront of our meetings, we can set up the expectation that we all are more cognizant of the way we speak about our students.

This is not an exercise that I would try at an all-staff meeting. If you are thinking globally or theoretically, you may lose different folks in the crowd who insist that they never do this or say these things. If you save this learning experience for a student data meeting, it puts a face and a name to the reflection of a specific student and allows more authentic reflection to occur.

There's a space for us to advocate and push thinking almost constantly, which is why our roles are so exhausting.

All kids have abilities, gifts, and talents. Our multilingual learners come to us with vast experiences, linguistic assets, and beautiful stories. They deserve our best. Let's advocate for our awesome kids and families!

A CALL TO ACTION

I hope that you find this book to be a call to action—no matter what role you have, no matter what type of school you serve, no matter how large or small your linguistically diverse student population is.

It is my hunch that the folks who take on this role of Change Agent often are the ones who find themselves on every committee at their school or in their district, so we'll discuss some of that, too. We understand that we need a seat at every table because our students, parents, and programs need a seat at every table.

Our roles encompass so much, but we start our work in the classroom.

MOVING BEYOND VIA REFLECTION & ACTION

Share out your reflections & action steps on Twitter using #MovingBeyondEdu

REFLECT:

- How does your school district identify linguistically diverse students? What does the label imply?
- What is an experience you've had that challenged you as a human being? What did you learn from it? What is an experience you've had that brought you immense joy? What did it teach you?
- What are some of your skills and talents? How about your passions? How can you invite them into your professional life?

ACT:

- Pay attention to the language choices you hear in the teachers' lounge, hallway, or at staff meetings. Is there an overabundance of "those kids," "her kids," "low kids," or "kids in that program?" Record your problematic language and write down positive alternatives. Point it out to your leaders and come up with a plan to bring this to folks' attention. Make a school goal around inclusive terminology and praise teachers and teams who make a conscious effort to shift their language choices to reflect inclusivity.

Instead of...	Let's try...

- Consider your spheres of influence. List out names of those you touch daily, weekly, and monthly in each of your circles. Is it larger than you thought? What does this mean for you?

My team	
My school	
My district	
My social groups (friends, clubs, sports leagues, etc.)	
My professional groups	
My spiritual groups (faith organizations, volunteer groups, causes that you are connected to, etc.)	

- Now that you're stepping into your space as a change agent, what does it mean for you?

2

BEYOND THE BASICS

FOUNDATIONAL CONSIDERATIONS

*S*erving multilingual learners is not just a list of instructional strategies. There are some important foundational considerations that we need to reflect on and understand before (and perhaps, instead of) jumping to a list of strategies.

THE FOUR DOMAINS

There are four domains of language: reading, writing, listening, and speaking. Do a quick lesson check. Pick a lesson from this past week—did the lesson allow students to read, write, listen, and speak?

You may have heard this before, and I certainly experienced it as a student. In our primary school grades, it is well-known and widely accepted that every child is developing language skills. There are tons of conversation-based activities, songs, co-constructed writing activities, oral story-telling opportunities, and lots of word exploration and wordplay! As students move up the grades, however, this happens less and less. Students are expected to be at a certain level of language usage. There is a misconception that songs are babyish and we need to move to more "academic" learning styles to prepare kids for the next grade level. We cut down on conversation time. By the time kids get to middle school or junior high, they are expected to be master listeners, "absorbing" everything that the speaker pours into the room.

I have to commiserate with our middle and secondary teachers here for a moment before moving on. There are tremendous pressures to cover content. There are a large number of standards and topics to explore. There is a pressure to go both deep and wide within each standard and unit. I get it.

However, there are easy ways to ensure that your lessons are incorporating all four domains of language and that each domain has identified supports that are accessible to anyone who may need it, including your monolingual speakers.

It is important to note that none of us teach content—we teach students. The content doesn't come first, the students do.

Most people who aren't EL teachers aren't used to planning lessons around the 4 domains of language, so this may be a shift. Depending on your block of time, the standards you are targeting, and the proficiency levels you currently have represented in your classroom, you can plan strategically for ways to incorporate all 4 domains in every lesson! Remember, this doesn't mean that each domain has the same number of instructional minutes or anything like that. This means that you are looking at your lesson through a language development lens.

Here are some important breakdowns to keep in mind:

Reading + Writing = Literacy
Listening + Speaking = Oracy
Reading + Listening = Receptive language (language one
receives)
Writing + Speaking = Expressive skills (language one
expresses)

Many times, folks will say that the receptive language skills come first (student input before student output). They'll also say that oracy comes before literacy. The most important thing for us to remember is that each language domain is *interconnected,* and there's no magical formula for the time it takes to develop in any one domain or set of domains. There's also no direct if/then correlation in proficiency skill development (for example, we wouldn't say that only when students are at a 3.3 receptive language level, would we focus instruction on expressive language skills). That said, there are best practices to use and consider when planning for instruction.

Both the **Sheltered Instruction Observation Protocol** (SIOP) and **Guided Language Acquisition Design** (GLAD) are two wonderful research-based frameworks from which to plan and instruct your lessons. I personally love SIOP. These would be great things for your school or district to look into, and not just for the EL, Bilingual, and/or Dual Language teachers on staff. It's for *everyone.* Language instruction occurs in every class throughout the day, so it's best for everyone when each educator owns that role and responsibility. The EL specialist can continue to dig into more specifically targeting language proficiencies, recommend appropriate scaffolds, and provide instructional guidance for content/classroom teachers.

One piece of instructional planning while utilizing the four domains include the idea of a language objective. Many of us hear this and we may break out in a rash, but I'm here to tell you not to panic. Your rash may be because of how content objectives or learning targets were launched in your school district. Were you mandated to have a bulletin board of objectives? Were you required to submit lesson plans with a bunch of state standard acronyms? Did you have to write them in teacher language, student-friendly language, and parent-friendly language?

When my district rolled it out, administrators would walk around the school and do pop-ins on lessons with their trusty iPads. For the first year, they would walk around and see if they could visibly locate the target posted somewhere in the room. If it was there, they'd write the target into their iPad. The following year, they asked students to recite the learning target. Many times, kids knew where to look in the classroom to find their target. That info also went into their Trusty Administrator iPad. Finally, they'd come in, record the target, and then ask the students more questions: *What is your learning target today? How will you know you've mastered it?* Oftentimes, they'd accidentally pick the student with the most anxiety, and get the answer of quiet sweating. All the data was recorded (in The Cloud? A Cloud? A hidden data pool in the sky?) and that was that.

So, if you're panicking, let me set the record straight. It's not about posting an additional target. It's not about your classroom walls or posters. It's not about worksheets. It's about marrying *the what* with *the how*. YOU are the educator, so you get to decide how that looks in the way that makes the most sense to you.

Our content objectives represent the subject area (science, physical education, visual art, math) and the language objective represents how students will engage with language via listening, reading, writing, and/or speaking. Dr. José Medina is a leading dual language researcher, author, and speaker—and he always says that writing a content objective without a language objective is like asking kids to find a target in the dark! Also, be sure you follow him on Twitter at @JoseMedinaJr89!

As we plan for instruction, we must always provide opportunities for students to engage in all four language domains as much as possible. There's a printable tool that I created using Google Images (feel free to use mine, utilize the QR code, or create your own!).

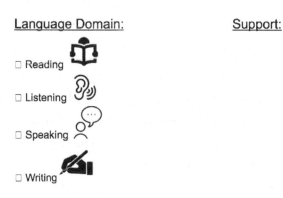

The above image is a teacher planning doc. This is a great tool to print, laminate, and use as a checklist in instructional planning. It has a visual for each domain along with space for built-in support . The second part of the tool (continued on the subsequent pages) is the very same visuals, just on a larger scale. It would be great to print this tool in the color of your choice, laminate, and post above your whiteboard or instructional space. That way, when you're instructing, you have a constant visual reminder to walk through the language domains for today's lessons with your students.

This would pair quite nicely with introducing your content objective or learning target. Let's imagine this in action, shall we?

> Teacher: Alright, mathematicians, future solvers of the world's problems. Today, we're going to tackle this learning target: I can add fractions with a common denominator. WOW! That's a big one. I'm so glad you are ready for this!

> Students: *Salivating over the chance to do hard math work* YAY! We love fractions! Denominators are endless fun!

> Teacher: Well, future engineers, designers, and CEOs. You may be wondering how we're going to do this. How are we possibly going to accomplish this in just 37 minutes? I'm so glad you asked! First, we're going to start by having a partner discussion and review what a denominator is, so we'll be listening and speaking with our partner (*point to the listening and speaking visuals*). Next, we're going to be reading through a few practice problems on page 5 (*point to the reading visual*) and finally, we'll be writing out our answers. You'll notice #7 has space for you to explain how you solved the problem in writing (*point to the writing visual*).

> *End scene.*

Okay, okay, I know. This was probably a primary school example. Middle schoolers seldom shout "Yay! We love fractions!" ...or do they?

The point of this was to see how to talk to kids about their learning targets while also walking them through the ways they'll be engaging with language during the lesson. Remember that everyone is developing language in your classroom, even you. To truly develop the academic language skills needed to navigate the content, kids need the opportunity to stay in the classroom with their peers and have ample opportunities to read, write, listen, and speak about the content they're learning.

Try it out! Pose a provocative question, phrase, word, image, meme, GIF, or statement on the board to open your class. This serves multiple purposes: one, it provides a fun hook to your learners. It gets them thinking about how it relates to today's content, and it keeps them on their toes. Two, it gets them processing language around the topic. Allow them a minute to think quietly by themselves before having them engage in a task that is centered around two or more domains (reading, writing, listening, or speaking).

Remember, you don't necessarily have to plan a lesson that includes 15 minutes of each domain in isolation—that's not how language works! If you're speaking to your class for eight minutes and they're listening for those eight minutes, how will you set up for more opportunities for students to engage in speaking and writing?

THE JOINING OF CONTENT LEARNING & LANGUAGE LEARNING

Language is not learned in isolation. Language is a social construct. We need to engage with reading, writing, listening, and speaking *about something*. Content is taught *through* language. *This is why it's so critically important that all educators see themselves as language teachers, no matter what's on their teaching certificates.* We should always lean on the expertise of our EL-certified staff, but we cannot abdicate the responsibility of serving our multilingual learners due to a lack of a specific certification.

This is also why the role of many EL teachers is changing. Many districts are moving away from the small groups outside of class to having co-taught classes or more in-class support. Explicit instruction is still needed. Opportunities to engage with the language in low-stakes settings are still needed. However, there are still ways to embed these opportunities within the core classroom if the right structures are in place.

SERVICE DELIVERY FOR LANGUAGE LEARNERS

There are many models for providing instructional services to language learners, some of which include sheltered instruction, out of class support (many call this "pull out" support), in-class support (many call this "push-in"), and co-teaching. It is so important for us to understand the differences in these terms, especially around in-class support and co-teaching, because these two models are quite different, but the terms are mistakenly used interchangeably often.

Let's define some popular models:

- In-class support: this occurs when a specialist comes into the classroom to provide additional support, reinforcement, or enrichment to targeted students
- Out-of-class support: this occurs when a specialist removes a student or group of students to provide additional support, reinforcement, or enrichment
- Co-Teaching: this occurs when a specialist partners with a classroom teacher to provide all learners with

additional support, reinforcement, or enrichment within the same space

CO-TEACHING

Co-teaching includes multiple components—and if any of these are missing, it is not true co-teaching. Co-teaching includes co-planning, co-instructing, co-assessing, and co-reflecting. If any of these components is missing, then it may be just some highly effective in-class support.

One such structure that must be in place is the people. Yes, I said it. The right educators with the right mindsets have to be there. If there is a classroom teacher who insists that Room 9 is *her classroom* and doesn't believe in the power of co-teaching, or who says things like "*I think it'd be easier if you just pulled them...*" then we have to unpack this a bit.

1. Let's discuss—It'd be *easier on who*? Are we in the business of doing things out of teacher convenience? Is this a student-centered decision?

2. Let's consider why someone might be feeling this way.

a. Has this teacher been burned in the past by an unsuccessful co-teaching situation? Are they simply burned out and don't feel like they can take on "one more thing?" They may not know how co-teaching or in-class support can benefit *all* students with enhanced instruction.

b. Has this teacher had the opportunity to be involved in co-teaching yet in their career? Are there experiences that they've had that make them weary to try it now?

c. Have the two teachers had an opportunity to get to know each other? Collaboration involves a level of getting to know the other adults in the room. Is one particularly passionate about math? Is one particularly good with an app like Seesaw? How can the teachers maximize their collective expertise and build on each other's passions?

d. Has the district provided the necessary professional learning to truly understand co-teaching and all that it entails? Is there ongoing support for this model of service?

Co-teaching is a journey, and it is absolutely one worth taking. It is important that there is support for co-teaching partnerships in schools via quality professional development and coaching opportunities. For further information, I would highly recommend exploring more about powerful co-teaching practices by reading *Collaborating for English Learners: A Foundational Guide to Integrated Practices* by Dr. Andrea Honigsfeld and Maria G. Dove (Corwin 2019).

INTERVENTIONS

Since the onset of Response to Intervention (RTI) structures and programs over the last decade, a lot of attention has been given to what type of program would fill what types of gaps. Many times, EL students are lumped into programs that were never designed with them in mind. These boxed programs are often linguistically limited in their scope, and when students use these programs for six to eight weeks and don't show the progress that monolingual students show, everyone assumes there's a learning disability. If we are focusing our efforts on programs instead of practices, we are missing the mark not just for multilingual students, but all students. If we are subjecting our students to drill and kill programs instead of highly engaging learning experiences, why are we so surprised when students stop engaging?

We have to keep language proficiency in mind when we are assigning students to interventions. If students are still developing in their language, is it appropriate to assign them to an intervention that was designed for monolingual students who have a noted need? Other thoughts to consider would be who is delivering the intervention (are they well-versed in language development, linguistic scaffolds, etc.?) and if the intervention program is linguistically appropriate for students.

We have to consider how students are identified for interventions. Are you using at least three *appropriate* data sets? Are you including multilingual data and information? Or, is your data set the same for every monolingual as well as multilingual students? How are you including English proficiency data in decision-making for intervention placement? Is the team soliciting feedback from all adults who touch the child—including the parents, and including the EL specialist?

When EL students are given interventions, depending on how interventions are set up in your system and what the intervention entails, it can increase gaps. For example, if your school setting has students missing fine arts classes or science/social studies content lessons to attend an Intervention... we are creating gaps. Let me be clear—we aren't creating *achievement gaps*, we are creating *opportunity gaps*. We aren't allowing our ELs to engage with those needed content areas—they aren't given the opportunity to learn the experience (much less the language) of the fine arts, social studies, or science. If our students are in an Intervention of some sort, what are they missing? If your school system has an intervention system set up where no students are missing new learning (or an entire content area), you may be in a better place than many!

You must also be considerate of what data will be used to determine if this intervention is working. Language development does not fit nicely into a six to eight week interval of instructional time, so if you are determining that a "deficit" has not been filled in a short window of time, and you're ready to move on to evaluating students for a potential disability, you may want to slow down.

For so many of us, our school districts went into hyperdrive in getting RTI systems set up, and now we are revisiting that framework and shifting into a Multi-Tiered System of Support (MTSS) structure that provides more than one way to support students. We can use this as a great opportunity to make sure that our structures, programs, and policies are linguistically appropriate and responsive to our students' abilities and needs.

Finally, please remember that language instruction is not an "intervention": it is a service that ensures students have access to their grade level content with their grade level peers. Language support should be happening in Tier One (and across every tier).

PROGRAM DIFFERENCES AND INTERRUPTED PROGRAMMING

The terms **Students with Limited or Interrupted Formal Education** (SLIFE) and **Students with Interrupted Education** (SIFE) are being discussed more in our field as we are growing our knowledge across the field about this specific group of learners, and I'm thankful for EL leaders like Carol Salva, author of *Boosting Achievement*, who provides us with great thinking and tools to support our students with interrupted formal education.

But what about *interrupted programming*?

I live and serve in the Chicagoland suburbs. We are an area blessed with rich linguistic diversity. Because the number of English Learners is so high, we have a variety of program models serving our students across each town and each school district. In one school district, we may see a two-way dual language program where the class consists of native language speakers and native English speakers, with the goal of biliteracy. In other districts, we may see a one-way dual language program with all native language speakers. In almost every school district, we see English Learner programs (transitional programs of instruction) with the goal of English language proficiency. Still, in others, we see transitional bilingual programs where we are leveraging two languages with the ultimate goal of English proficiency, and we follow language allocation plans that gradually increase the usage of English. There are so many models out there, and districts arrive at those programs in different ways in the hopes of supporting their linguistically diverse student populations.

However, what happens when one student transfers out of the school that offers a one-way dual language program and enters a school with a transitional program of instruction? The goals of those two models are completely different—the language of instruction is different. It is important to have a rich dialogue between the previous school and new school so that the program goals are clearly explained.

An articulation meeting should be set up so that the new school can understand the differences in programming. This is important because if a student is accustomed to using a home language for half of their instructional day, they may not yet have the vocabulary to access the content in English only. The instructional team (including the EL specialist, classroom teacher, and related student services staff) needs to be aware so that they don't impart deficit-lens thinking onto the student. This way we can avoid the whole ugly conversation, "But they were born here. Why don't they know these science words yet? There must be a disability. They're so discrepant."

DUALLY IDENTIFIED STUDENTS

Students who are dually identified (meaning that they have an IEP and are also identified as EL) need all service providers at the table when making decisions on programming. What seems to happen in many school districts, especially with schools that are larger in student population, is that there is a cluster of EL students within one grade-level team of teachers and a separate cluster of IEP students on another team of teachers. Typically, this is done to maximize services with a limited number of specialists available. The argument is that it is easier to collaborate with four adults and across four classrooms instead of stretching a specialist too thin by collaborating with eight adults and across eight classrooms. What happens though, when we have students who fall on both teams?

We need to be thoughtful of the ways that we are providing support to our dually identified students. Of course, I'll recommend that you turn to your state agencies for your specific guidelines, but here is my reminder that EL Specialists are a member of the IEP team also. The EL Specialist has formative assessment data, language proficiency data, anecdotal data, and more to share with the team. They know which linguistic scaffolds to provide and recommend. They know how to create an IEP goal that matches the student's linguistic abilities and helps them to level up. Be sure these folks are at the table as goals are written! Special education services do not "trump" EL services—ever. Both services are a right of the student, and both must be provided.

TRANSITIONING STUDENTS

As we end each school year, it is a common practice for us to meet with next year's teachers and share goals, plans, and needs. We must establish and revisit any language norms for the conversations we have and the statements we make about students. We especially need to be critical of this as we talk about plans and goal-setting for the next school year. As teachers gather around the table, push yourself to *only* share the gifts and talents of our kids. Avoid making lists of all the ways the student isn't at the same level as someone else. Allow next year's teacher to form their professional analysis of the student.

From the Blog: Allowing our EL Students a Fresh Start Next Year

Does your school or district have a system for passing on words of wisdom and tidbits to the next teacher, especially if you work in a smaller system where you happen to know next year's teachers? What are your thoughts on the process?

What's helpful to share about students for their next teacher:
*Their passions, interests, and talents
*Some instructional and assessment data, including language proficiency data
*A language profile
*Strong scaffolds that have worked well
*Personal insights (what the student may find upsetting, what brings the student joy, any other information that might impact the student's wellness, social-emotional learning, or academic learning)

What's not helpful to share about students for their next teacher:

*Their behavior: unless the student is on a formal behavior plan, the student is going to a new teacher in just months from now. Allow the new teacher to form a relationship without preconceived notions in their head.

*Judgements about their family: avoid the phrases "there's no support at home" or "the family is not involved." You are an educator, not a parenting judge. Your definition of "support at home" and "family involvement" is not the end-all-be-all... and it's not the same for every family.

By allowing next year's teacher a blank slate, you are allowing the teacher to make their own determinations about what works best. A new school year and a new relationship with a new adult doesn't need to be tainted with last year's behavior log or one teacher's judgment of the family. Next year's teacher will have fresh eyes, fresh experiences, and a fresh relationship to build with their new student. Let's set them up for success, free of our judgment. By all means, pass along what the teacher needs to know—but by allowing our colleagues the opportunity for that fresh start, we are setting everyone up for success.

THE TIME IT TAKES

Jim Cummins has spoken about Basic Interpersonal Communication Skills (BICs) and Cognitive Academic Language Proficiency (CALPS) since 1979. Perhaps you've seen the iceberg image before that describes the language skills we can "see" versus the language we can deeply understand. Think back to someone you know who talks about their study-abroad experience or their trip to another country and how excited they were to order a drink at the restaurant in the language they were trying to navigate—that's BICs. Now let's revisit the bookshelf directions written in another language—that's CALPs. BICs and CALPs have different functions but students can and do develop both simultaneously.

Many folks will be so impressed with students who are within their first year of navigating a new language. They'll marvel at how quickly the student can acquire language. Our students are amazing, no doubt! *But,* this often places an unrealistic expectation/demand on the student as they move up in proficiency levels.

I love the movie *Legally Blonde*. One of my favorite scenes is when Elle Woods takes her friend Paulette to get her dog back from her ex-husband. Elle plays with technical vocabulary from law school that she hasn't yet mastered in the scene. Luckily, the ex-husband isn't familiar with any of the legal jargon, so he doesn't notice, and Elle and Paulette rejoice when they get the dog back.

Elle Woods is fluent in English. Though the storyline doesn't explicitly say it, many might assume that she spoke English her whole life, but during that specific scene, it was obvious that she wasn't *yet* proficient in the technical language of law school. I wonder if her law professors were worried about her learning and recommended that she receive an IEP?

Woah, that sounded a bit dramatic, huh? Well...

To get right down to it, the linguistic demand moves upward and outward as students grow in their language proficiency. An increasing amount of academic language is needed (in reading, writing, listening, and speaking) as the student "levels up." So what we often say about the student changes very quickly when we see the student begin to slow in their progression. Because the linguistic demand increases, we often see "slower" progress as students move higher up the proficiency scale. We start to panic and wonder what's wrong.

Very often, we will become frustrated at the perceived-slow growth at the higher proficiency levels. We are shocked when the students stop growing as quickly as they once had. We start to make assumptions, hypotheses, and recommendations before we even start "beefing up" the linguistic supports at Tier 1.

Another interesting thing to note here is that many EL programs focus a lot of energy around providing supports based on proficiency. For example, students who are at the beginning stages of language development receive the most instructional support (via in-class support, out-of-class support, sheltered instruction, or co-teaching). As students grow, the supports are often scaled back. This begs the question, how are we creating meaningful instructional supports at *all* levels of proficiency?

Every proficiency level is different, and there are great instructional supports that we can use to scaffold learning at each level and in each domain.

STUDENTS WHO WERE ONCE ELS

Students who exit EL programs must continue to be monitored by teachers to ensure that they are still able to navigate the academic language across content areas. Each state has different exit criteria based on language proficiency assessments, so all teachers must be familiar with their state's policies.

It's important to note that each state's set of exit scores does not imply proficiency across all four domains of language. For example, in the state of Illinois at the time of this writing, students must receive a 4.8 composite score on their ACCESS test. (The ACCESS test is the annual assessment that students in K-8 for identified multilingual learners in any WIDA state.) The state currently does not require a certain proficiency level in reading or writing; it's a general composite of the four domains. The states stop providing Title III funds for students who have reached their "exit" score—so, many school districts will cut services to those students because they've exited their EL programs. However, under ESSA, states are now required to continue to monitor EL students' progress even after they exit their EL programs.

We have to remember that even if a student has "exited" their state's program because they reached a certain score threshold, it doesn't mean that they've mastered all of the language nuances across each domain of reading, writing, listening, and speaking. Students may still require (and they are still entitled to) support to navigate grade level content.

SIMULTANEOUS VS. SEQUENTIAL

For some multilingual students, they are raised in one country with one language, and then they move to the US and begin their journey of acquiring English. This is called Sequential Bilingualism: one language happens first, and then another begins. For most multilingual students in the US today, students are raised in the US and they are growing up learning and growing in two languages. This is called Simultaneous Bilingualism. What's important and beautiful here is this: there is no one way to acquire language.

The danger comes when we start labeling our simultaneous bilingual learners as one of the following:

- That student doesn't have a dominant language
- They are low/weak in both languages
- They don't have a command of either language
- They're confusing their languages

Allowing our students to embrace their linguistic assets honors their identities, their families, their cultures, their skills, and their ability to be themselves fully and wholly. There are assessments we can use and anecdotal pieces of data that we can collect to help us understand levels of proficiency in various languages, but we know that no one piece of data can capture our students' full linguistic scope of skills, and our holistic lens of our students should never be based on what the student hasn't yet mastered.

BEWARE OF THE BOX (PROGRAMS)

I'm generally not a fan of "programs" and kits of resources. I much prefer to prioritize *practices* over *programs*. I don't think kids learn best from boxes; I think they learn best from exciting content taught by passionate educators. I'm always especially wary of publishers who claim to have resources to support biliteracy for bilingual or dual language programs.

In my local area, the most popular language for bilingual and dual language programs is Spanish, and for that reason, I am going to use Spanish as the example here. *Biliteracy is NOT English literacy in Spanish*. Resources that are translated through technology do not impress me. Also, resources that are just mere translations of the English sources are okay, but I much prefer authentic Spanish texts. These are texts that were originally written in Spanish. Bilingual books where we see both languages side by side are also good, depending on the quality of the translation.

If you are monolingual and you are in charge of ordering or choosing materials to support your literacy programs (or any program really), there are certain things that you should do and ask prior to signing the check.

1. Please check in with your bilingual staff—you know, those folks who are actually teaching for biliteracy. You

can certainly tap the opinions of your coaches and administrators, but it is critical to get the feedback, experience, and expertise of the educators who are teaching it. Ensure that the educators have a firm understanding of biliteracy instruction and how to navigate the three linguistic spaces in their instruction. Consider your language allocation plan and see if the materials are a good match for your program. You may wish to consider running a pilot of the program prior to investing in it. Don't make a decision for your school district based on how it serves 80% of the students. Focus also on the 20% most vulnerable students. This way you'll reach everyone.

2. Ask the right questions of the publisher. Here are some to consider. If there are materials in another language:

3. Are they translations of the English resources? Who (or what) translated them? How does the publisher ensure that the translations are high quality?

4. Are *all* components of the program translated into other languages? Or just certain components? Oftentimes, publishers overlook the supplementary materials and only provide translations of the "biggest" pieces. Do their translations include subtitles, graphics, tables, charts, homework, videos, audio clips, and teacher tools? If not, please remember: this means that someone will have to translate all of these things.

5. Are the materials in another language based on English Language Arts Standards, or something different? For example, if the materials are to support Spanish/English biliteracy, did the publisher consult any Spanish Language Arts Standards?

6. Who at the publishing company has taught for

biliteracy? Who was involved in the development of the bilingual resources?

While we're on this topic, please note that while workshops and PD offerings are great for monolingual staff, don't assume that attendance at one workshop (or a series of workshops) is the same level of expertise of actually having an EL/Bilingual endorsement as well as teaching experience. Involve your experts in decision-making whenever possible.

MOVING BEYOND VIA REFLECTION & ACTION

Share out your reflections & action steps on Twitter using #MovingBeyondEdu
REFLECT:

- Whose responsibility is it to teach language? How can you share this message with your building to nurture a culture of shared responsibility?
- In what ways do you articulate with the next grade levels' teachers regarding students you serve? What are key pieces of information that are necessary to share?

ACT:

- In what ways do you check your instruction to ensure you are incorporating all four domains of language?

How will I provide time for listening?	How will I provide time for speaking?	How will I provide for reading?	How will I provide time for writing?
Activity:	Activity:	Activity:	Activity:
Scaffold:	Scaffold:	Scaffold:	Scaffold:

- Have a trusted colleague come in and observe your lesson to check your domain usage. How many minutes were students reading, writing, speaking, and listening? Ask them to pick a student and tally the minutes for you.

LISTENING	SPEAKING	READING	WRITING
Time:	Time:	Time:	Time:
Notes:	Notes:	Notes:	Notes:

3

BEYOND VISUALS

STRATEGIES THAT SUPPORT

This idea of moving beyond visuals strikes a chord with me every time I attend a conference (and I *love* attending conferences).

There's usually a section of large conferences dedicated to publishers, allowing them to share their resources and materials. It's a great opportunity to see what's out there, what's new, what's changed, and meet some reps who can talk to your district leadership about how their resources can support your students. I love seeing what's out there and I love meeting new people.

Something unnerving happens at many of those tables, though. I walk by, perusing materials that are organized by grade level, genre, or (when I'm lucky) language or proficiency level—and there's always this one thing I see.

I'll usually see it in big, bright colorful letters. They're surrounded by a giant word bubble. If this were Vegas, there would be a blinking, neon sign, too. You've probably seen this, too. Here it is: — GREAT FOR LANGUAGE LEARNERS, TOO —

This is great from a marketing lens, I'm guessing. The bright colors draw the eye. The phrase itself I find problematic, but more on that in a moment. It probably gets folks walking by to stop at the publisher's table, which is where the fun begins.

I imagine the scene unfolding like a bad-dream sequence in my head. Here's how it plays out:

Teacher: Oh hello, I see your resources are great for language learners! I serve many in my classroom. Can you tell me about it?

Publisher: YES, come on down! We have found the secret sauce! This is going to blow your mind. We cannot wait for you to see it!

Teacher: Wow, really? That's fantastic! Tell me all about it!

Publisher: Well, you see these materials here? Check this out. *Pulls out sample packages.* This is what the student will see when you begin the lesson. Here's your script for every word you'll say.

Teacher: *Nods, smiles, perhaps questions why they need a script if they're not acting in a play.*

Publisher: Now, here's where it gets really good! You're going to LOVE this. On this page is the lesson plan. We've broken this particular lesson down into 17 easy steps. This is how you'll teach everyone else. On this side of the page, you'll notice a list of all the materials and page numbers you'll need. THEN, *eyes widen, voice lowers* you'll note that every single lesson plan has this VERY HELPFUL box over here. Can you read it for me?

Teacher: This small, gray box? It says "For Language Learner Supports."

Publisher: *Excitedly claps hands.* YES! Every lesson features this magical box! It tells you exactly how to modify the lesson to teach your language learners!

Teacher: *Squints eyes to focus on the text in the ugly gray box.* It says "*use visuals.*"

Publisher: YES! ISN'T THAT GENIUS?

Teacher: *Flips pages, sees that all lessons have the same ugly gray box with the same pieces of advice.*

End scene,

Have you experienced this before? Now, before my publisher buddies throw things at me, I realize that not all publishers do this, and many do have wonderful resources and materials. But friends, if this feels familiar to you, can we talk about this?

When folks declare "this works for _____, too" — this phrase is problematic. This implies that any student group other than a majority (and perhaps privileged) group is viewed through a deficit lens. As in: "Wow, this resource will even work for *them.*" Ugh. Also, if you're creating lessons that you have admitted were *only* designed for a majority, I'm not interested. If you have something that you've poured so much time and money into creating and producing and marketing, but you didn't address my students first, that means that you left them as an afterthought, so I'm not interested.

When publishers (or anyone else—coaches, leaders, consultants, etc.) declare that they have the singular answer to serving all linguistically diverse students, that's problematic. Our students are not one-size-fits-all. There is no singular answer to serving anyone. Every child is complex and has unique needs and experiences. It is up to the art and science of the educator to determine the need and provide whatever supports and scaffolds are most meaningful.

OF COURSE, visuals *are* a powerful scaffold to increase comprehensible input, but that can't be our end-all-be-all answer. Visuals are one piece of support, and not all visuals are meaningful. We can all absolutely move beyond visuals.

MULTILINGUAL LEARNERS ARE NOT A HOMOGENOUS GROUP!

It is critical that we understand that multilingual learners as a student group are not homogenous. Every student has a different story! What works for one multilingual learner may not work for others in your class. Each student has a different experience in their heritage language. Just because they can speak and listen in another language doesn't automatically mean they have literacy skills in their native language. Just because a family member speaks one language doesn't mean the children in the home speak the language. Students have varying levels of native language proficiency across domains. They also have differing passions, talents, skills, and interests. Some are visual learners while others are kinesthetic. Each student has varying levels of education if they come from another country. I've heard students express frustration with how "slow-moving" math is in the US while another student from a different country expressed annoyance with the amount of reading and writing in US math. Still another suggested that math was too hard for this particular grade level. So please remember that while strategies will be explored in this chapter, it is important for us to note that these are tools for your toolboxes, but it is so important to get to know our students as learners!

THE STRATEGIC USE OF SCAFFOLDS

Scaffolds matter—and they should match the purpose, the content, the expectation, the content task, and the language necessary to navigate the learning. *Strategic* scaffolds are critical. This shouldn't be a pre-selected drop-down from a menu type of decision. Many times, EL teachers advise classroom teachers on what types of scaffolds are commonly used for certain proficiency levels, which is very helpful to educators who do not have EL accreditation and training. However, it is important to carefully select the scaffold to support the specific type of learning taking place. Ideally, these types of decisions would be made in collaboration with a content teacher. This allows a great conversation to take place that builds the skills of both educators!

Scaffolds are meant to be *temporary* supports. If you consider the way painters will build scaffolds to reach the higher parts of the wall, you'll note that once the higher parts of the walls are painted, they take the scaffolds down. They remove them—they've served their purpose! Like painters, we again are encouraged to be strategic in the way we lessen/remove scaffolds, layer by layer.

PRACTICES THAT BENEFIT ALL

I believe that powerful practices can really transform our instruction and make learning more accessible to all learners. There is a saying in our field that many of these instructional shifts and strategies are "good for all, but necessary for multilingual learners." If all of us are developing in our language, and we consider our instruction through a language lens, then *everyone* benefits.

LEVEL UP

There have been many studies shown about the low-level tasks that many of our language learners are tasked with across various content. In the book *Breaking Down The Wall* (2019) by Espino Calderón, Dove, Staehr Fenner, Gottlieb, Honigsfeld, Ward Singer, Slakk, Soto, and Zacarian, an entire chapter is devoted to raising the expectations we have for our kids. We cannot water down content learning for students and expect students to ever access grade-level content independently.

I remember being taught in my undergraduate education courses to make work less overwhelming for students who are struggling by cutting their workload in half. If the assignment asks students to complete 30 problems, instead assign 15 problems. Unfortunately, we never discussed how to choose the 15 problems kids are asked to do. Many "challenge" or critical thinking problems are at the bottom of the pages (for whatever reason), so if we simply chop the assignment in half from the middle of the page down, our students lose out on the opportunity to even attempt the critical thinking problems. Therefore, we should analyze, then prioritize which problems on the page we ask students to do. We can also ask ourselves if worksheets are the best way to teach the concept?

My colleague Sarah Said, Director of Language and Equity Programs at Elgin Math and Science Academy (you can find her on Twitter @MrsSaid17), led a session at the Multilingual Illinois Conference in 2019 where she said that educators should always "Level UP and never water down." She shared that she never modifies the text that the students are asked to engage with or read. More specifically about the strategic use of scaffolds, she said, "Don't modify down, but scaffold up!" I loved this advice!

AFFECTIVE FILTER

We can maintain the rigor but also lower the stakes. We must consider ways for us to lower the affective filter! The affective filter refers to Stephen Krashen's work that originated in 1986 which taught us that learning can occur better when we are not stressed. Sometimes, we don't realize how intimidating certain language tasks can be! Create a culture of "playing with language," and be vulnerable about sharing your mistakes, like when you misspell something on a slide or a poster. We all make "mistakes" with language; it's natural!

Pose a question. This isn't new, right? Put the question in writing and display it on your screen or board, and also read it aloud. You've now incorporated 2 domains already, as the students are now reading and listening. Now, turn your back on your class or close your eyes (this is the part where the teachers who have students over the age of 11 are thinking, "HAVE YOU NEVER TAUGHT MIDDLE SCHOOL?!") and announce to the class, "Here is our question, but I'm not calling on anyone for 20 seconds." When you say this in front of kids without physically turning your back on them, you will always have those 3-5 students who stare you down to make eye contact with you so that you can see their hand up. Or, when they're especially excited, their hands will be up with fingers wiggling and an occasional "Ooh, ooh!" will escape their mouths. For this reason, I encourage you to turn your back, move away from your kids, or close your eyes (or make a fake attempt to cover your eyes). This will decrease the number of kids with anxious hands in the air.

After those 20 seconds are up, face your class once more and say, "Okay, now that we've had a moment to think about the answer, whisper the answer to your hands." Instruct kids to cover their mouths and whisper aloud what they think. You can also have them turn to talk to the wall, the floor, the inside of their elbow, etc. If you're doing this in a small group setting at a kidney table, have them turn towards the outside of the table and whisper it.

Then announce to the students, "Go ahead and check your answer with the person sitting next to you." Now they're excited to have someone to talk to, and you give whichever student feels more confident the chance to share first.

Now ask the partners to check in with another set of partners. Allow them to share their answer or their partner's answers. The group may or may not reach consensus on the answer, but now they've had a few folks to check their thinking.

Finally, ask for someone to share their thoughts or an idea of a classmate. You will have many more hands than just cold-calling. You've given everyone a chance to lower the Affective Filter. You've created a low-stakes opportunity to share thinking and lighten the linguistic load by providing oral rehearsal time.

You probably won't do this for every question you pose, but allowing kids multiple chances to practice expressing their thinking can be helpful. It gives kids a low-stakes opportunity to try out their word choice, phrasing, grammar, etc. Hearing a peer talk about the topic allows students to hear the ways that they engage in language around the content. It can also allow kids to "borrow" the language they heard (or confirm or correct any incorrect word choices/grammar that they may have had). An authentic conversation around content is much more meaningful, more relevant, and provides more immediate feedback than any worksheet. This can be done through asynchronous remote learning as well through video/audio messaging or apps like Flipgrid.

If we are instructing remotely and our students are connected to us online, we should consider that some students may feel stressed turning their screens on for instruction. If stress levels are high, meaningful learning cannot occur. By allowing students to choose an image, change their virtual background, or just showing their ceilings, we can be respectful of students' privacy and also encourage a sense of safety.

CORRECTING STUDENTS' LANGUAGE USAGE

While we can recognize ways for us to lower the affective filter during our instruction, we should also consider how we can offer corrective feedback to students while honoring their language development and respecting the time, space, and play needed to learn language. When students offer a statement with incorrect syntax or grammar, we can reinforce language patterns without shaming or humiliating learners. My daughter is a monolingual language learner, and while my son is in charge of the laundry at home, she is in charge of sweeping and vacuuming the floors. I love when she grabs the broom—she will often announce that she is *brooming*. I can honor her language choice and even praise her language play of taking the noun *broom* and turning it into a verb! I can also supply her with the word *sweeping*. If we talk about why she made the language choice "brooming," we can explore how her brain is thinking through language and how she is taking rules that she knows and is trying it out with a different word. So cool!

ORACY

Bad news, teachers. The lecture-only method called me. It wants to return to the 1970s.

I don't know about you, but I don't like professional learning that's "sit and get." I hate sitting in chairs listening to one speaker (no matter how engaging they are) for 60 minutes (or longer, ugh!). I check out. I scroll on my phone, answer a few text messages, or read my email. Luckily, I don't have to endure much of those any more these days, as folks do have a better understanding of how adults learn best. They know that adults like to have "think time," and they appreciate the time to talk and process through content with a peer or colleague. Their butts and backs hurt after sitting for too long without getting up. They don't enjoy listening to someone who lacks passion. For many, ice breaker activities are annoying. My personal least favorite is when the speaker "invites" the room to get up and talk to someone you don't normally work with each day—as my son says, it's "cringey" for me.

The fact is, kids often share many of the same learning preferences as us. They don't enjoy "sit and get" content. They hate listening with no breaks for 60-minute blocks of time. And yes, they get uncomfortable sitting in those awful chairs that long, too. This is one reason why I like flexible seating options.

As students move into the upper grades, they have significantly fewer opportunities to engage in conversations about the content; however, there are easy ways for all of us to incorporate more oracy into our classrooms. Here are a few of those ways.

- Build in the use of sentence stems for students as they engage in conversations.
- *Ex: I agree with Juliana because _____. I disagree*

with Jonathan because I believe _____. Research shows _____.

- Explicitly teach ways to build on conversations (follow-up questions, rephrase the speaker, ask clarifying questions, respond, etc.) and share ways that folks are often conversation killers (one-word answers, one-word responses, etc.).
- Avoid the "find someone you don't normally work with" approach to partnering up. Try using Student Sorting Sticks to quickly assign random pairings or groupings so that you can maximize your instructional time.
- Strategically partner students of varying levels of proficiency.
- Encourage students to "speak with their hands" in addition to their voices.
- Throw away your Voice Level chart. Loud classrooms are often indicators of more student engagement (but not always, of course—but I'm hoping you will embrace a noisier learning space).
- Set timers to maximize instructional minutes and to allow the continuous flow of the lesson. You don't have to stick to them by the second, but it helps as you begin to plan lessons around including opportunities for each language domain.

COMPREHENSIBLE INPUT

I cannot build things to save my life. I admit it. I can buy the most simplistic bookshelf in the world from Target, take the box home, lay out all the pieces, find the directions, and still not know what to do. This is why I'll gladly shop garage sale sites and inherit hand-me-down (i.e., pre-made) furniture instead, or ask my husband to build things for me. It's just not a strong skill I possess.

Next time you are tasked with putting together a bookshelf, take a peek at the instructions and note the way the company tries to help you understand. Generally, there is a listing of all the materials and parts. Often there are tiny stickers on the objects themselves so that you know for certain that you're using the right pieces in the directions. They break things down step-by-step and often use numbers: Step 1, Step 2, etc.

Almost always, there are visuals. I want you to analyze the visuals. How do they help you? Are there arrows to show what goes where? If you are multilingual, do you check in with a set of directions in your additional language? Do you find sometimes that the written directions with visuals are not enough and you must resort to looking on YouTube to watch it being done? Is there a phone number to call or a website to visit for more help?

I'd like you now to analyze this situation if fewer supports were given and more restrictions were in place. The new restrictions include:

- *No visuals*
- *Written directions in paragraph format*
- *No talking to a partner or group of peers while you're working on this*
- *No videos*
- *Work by yourself*
- *Turn in your final product without receiving any support or feedback*

How would your bookshelf look under all these circumstances?

I'm afraid these are all too familiar scenarios that we find in many classrooms. Students are less encouraged to talk things through with a partner, and looking on YouTube for additional help is considered "cheating."

All of these additional layers that we may have found helpful are examples of comprehensible input. These are things that help us make sense of the content we're learning, whether it's building a bookshelf from Target or understanding the solar system. Let's talk through some of these pieces of comprehensible input.

SUPPORTIVE IMAGES

As I said, yes—*visuals are great*, but let's dive deeper. If I'm reading about the elaborate names of the teeny, tiny parts of a stapler, and you show me a picture of a stapler, that may not help me in my understanding. Is this going to help me acquire the names of the tiny parts? How do I know which part of the stapler is which? Arrows and labels may help me understand better.

The quality of the photo matters and it must match the purpose of the content and task. It must match what the learner needs to navigate the content.

We have millions of images at our fingertips all time, and there's no excuse to not embed some helpful visuals into our lessons. Teach with your phone in your pocket or an iPad on your table—always have a device nearby, so you can quickly find an image online to enhance understanding. Allow and encourage students to look up images when needed.

RATE OF SPEECH

We need to slow down. Period. A slower rate of speech is a simple way to build more opportunities for comprehensible input. Most of us speak too quickly and for too long, which does not give our listeners' brains time to process, think, interpret, sort that information in their heads, and plan *to do something* with that information (respond, take notes, understand, or even more often—write, tell, create, etc). This doesn't mean that we need to speak at a disrespectfully slow rate to any of our students, but slowing down your speech is one easy way for us to build comprehensible input for all of the students we serve.

If this is a struggle for you, create a signal for yourself—whether it's putting a certain symbol in a Google Slides presentation that reminds you to pause or repeat information, or a water bottle that you hold in your hands so you remember to stop to take a sip thereby pausing your talking. This will slow your speech down for you.

And remember, *slower does not mean louder.*

TOTAL PHYSICAL RESPONSE (TPR)

Total Physical Response, or TPR, is a tool that many educators use that empowers learners to link a specific word to a gesture or movement. TPR can be used in a few different ways, depending on the purpose.

The power comes when the students have the opportunity to hear the word in context and have conversations about what the word means and doesn't mean. Then, students can co-create the movement or gesture to see the word in action.

At some times, educators may pre-designate a gesture or movement when they're just providing the word as exposure or to provide more comprehensible input. Other times, when the purpose is to have students interact and engage with a specific piece of vocabulary, it is more powerful for the students to create their own gestures or movement to accompany the word. This can be done in partners, small groups, or with the whole class, and it works for any content area!

For example, if I were teaching about the rotation of the planets, I may want to focus on the word rotate. I could pair the word *rotate* with the word *spin* for increased understanding, and I also could show what rotating is either by spinning my finger in a circle or by slowly spinning my body in a circle. Linking the word with an action is powerful (and fun—but don't get too dizzy rotating through science class)!

In a remote learning environment, I can take TPR to the next level by utilizing GIFs to demonstrate specific words. I can create my own by utilizing generators like the one Esther Park (find her on Twitter at @MrsParkShine) taught me about. You can find it online at www.andtheniwaslike.co!

VOCABULARY

We need to examine how we support vocabulary development by analyzing our instruction. We cannot teach words in isolation. If I'm reading words on a word list over and over again—no matter how many pretty color posters are up on the walls, I'm not going to learn what the words mean and how to use them if I don't get to interact with those words within context.

From content-specific vocabulary to technical vocabulary, to the academic language terms that I need to access across content areas, I need time to read, write, listen, and speak using those specific terms. I also need feedback to know if I'm using it correctly.

Many of us are fans of the hit Netflix series Schitts Creek, about a family who was once very affluent but had everything taken away from them when a trusted business partner made some poor financial decisions. There is a wonderfully humorous scene where two of the characters are cooking together. Moira, the mother, insists that she found an old recipe that she wants to pass down to her son, David. There was a step in the directions that said to "fold in the cheese." David asked his mother what that meant. Moira couldn't explain (she obviously didn't know either), so she insists that you "simply fold it in." David again states that he doesn't understand. He asks if that means you fold the cheese in half like a piece of paper. She dodges explaining the step over and over again until David leaves the kitchen at his wit's end.

What I love about this moment is that while David and Moira are both fluent English speakers, they both struggled with this specific use of the word *fold* because they were unfamiliar with the *context* of the word. Context matters!

BACKGROUND KNOWLEDGE

Growing up in the city of Chicago, my sisters and I were fascinated by "wildlife," which to us meant birds, squirrels, raccoons, possums, and rats. Sometimes we'd take drives to the suburbs or go fishing and we'd see magical creatures like rabbits, deer, and turtles. My husband still gets annoyed if we're driving around somewhere and happen to spot a deer because I absolutely freak out. He grew up outside of Columbus, Ohio, and spent summers in Pennsylvania, so our definitions of "rare wildlife" are quite different.

During the summers, my family and I would take week-long trips to West Virginia to visit my mom's family. We were infatuated with the mountains and forests. It was like being teleported to a whole new universe!

I became a mama in my early 20's, and when my son was little, we took a trip to visit my husband's family who lives in rural Pennsylvania. We took a short drive from PA to an outdoor adventure park in West Virginia. We had the diaper bag packed, fully stocked, I had my digital camera charged, and we were ready to go.

We stepped out of the car in the parking lot and started our walk into the park. That's when I first saw them.

I looked down. They were EVERYWHERE. I blinked a few times. I squinted to be sure that I was seeing correctly. Yes, indeed —they were what I thought they were: acorns.

I fell to my knees and let out a big yell: "OH MY GOOD-NESS! Babe, look!" I grabbed a whole bunch of them in my hand and held them up for him to see. If you ever met my husband, you'd knowingly nod here, because he's not very excitable. "Cool," was his reply. I instead turned towards my toddler son, who was equally as excited as I was (because *duh*, toddlers are always ready for a party).

I started to grab handfuls and stuffed them into my pockets and put a bunch in our diaper bag, too. *"My sisters aren't even going to believe this!"* I thought. I took out my flip phone and started to send text messages to my sisters—I JUST FOUND ACORNS. I AM BRINGING SOME HOME FOR YOU. I was admittedly a little dejected at their reply: LOL OKAY KISS BABY TJ FOR US.

The rest of the family kind of shrugged their shoulders at me but not a soul judged me for my excitement over these acorns. All of the sudden, it hit me—and I was so embarrassed.

Acorns were real. Of course. Everyone already knew that.

Except me—I just found out. I literally had *just learned* that acorns were a real thing. I spent my entire childhood watching Chip N' Dale episodes on old Disney VHS tapes. Do you know the ones? Chip N' Dale, the little mischievous chipmunks, would have quite the crazy adventures with Donald Duck. Being chip-munks, they would collect and hoard all their acorns.

I was 23 and I had never seen acorns in real life until this moment. My sisters, who grew up in the same house as me, who took the same family trips I had taken, were somehow able to understand that acorns were real, but I never got the message. I had a college education, but somehow that had never come up in school.

I tell this story because it's important to note a few things here. Various levels of background knowledge are not based on socioeconomic status. I cannot tell you how many times folks have said that a lack of background knowledge in a particular content area is related to a level of poverty. This is troubling for several reasons.

Whatever content/units we study in school was a choice. It was a decision made by a publisher, a group of policymakers who created the standards, or the educators who developed the units. Many times, those folks all look the same. Specifically, most are white and monolingual.

When anyone at the table declares that a student has "no background knowledge," please follow up with the question "*in what?*" There are so many topics in which I have limited or no background knowledge including planting, mechanics, chemistry, medicine, designing clothes, sewing, Wall Street, buying a Louis Vuitton bag, earthquakes, using a lawnmower, and countless other things. So should someone declare that I have "no background knowledge" or should they say "she has limited background knowledge with earthquakes;" which statement more accurately captures my background knowledge?

There is an assumption that because my background knowledge is different from others' background knowledge, it's *limited*. Here we go again, talking about the differences in asset-based lenses versus deficit-based lenses. We have some lens-flipping to do, don't we?

BUILDING BACKGROUND KNOWLEDGE

You can build background knowledge for everyone and level the playing field, so to speak. When I was in my undergraduate education classes, I remember being taught by my professors to end units of study with a culminating event: a video! A field trip! A science experiment! A talent show! A science fair!

However, to build background knowledge for all—and to give multilingual learners an experience to *engage in language* about— why don't we *start* our learning with these experiences? Launch the lesson with a video clip. Hook your kids with a science experiment that you can break apart and explain later. Take a virtual field trip (or a real field trip) to launch the social studies unit. You'll hit various learning styles (audio, visual, kinesthetic) and everyone will have something to build upon. You won't even have to degrade anyone's socioeconomic status in the process (insert eye roll here)! Win, win!

RELEVANCE

Is the instruction meaningful and relevant to our kids? Do they find value in the content?

Have you ever gone to a professional learning workshop, webinar, or conference and tuned completely out, thinking "*This does not apply to me*" or "*This doesn't make sense for the way my school functions.*" What happens after you make that personal determination? You shut off your listening because you're no longer invested. You might catch up on emails, text messages, or have a brain break, scroll through your social media feeds, play a quick game of something, etc. We do this all the time because our brains have a sorting system to organize information. If this isn't information that I will need, I can allow myself to save my energy for other things.

Kids have this system, too. If we can't show them that their learning is important, how can we become frustrated when they're not engaging with the content? We have to be able to find that bridge between creating lessons that are engaging but also relevant. They have to mean something for our students.

READING LIFE

If we want our students to love reading, then we have work to do. If our students have limited access to print, it's our job to break down those barriers and find ways to pour books into their lives. Garage sales, used book sales, warehouse sales, donations, wish lists, fundraisers, crowd-source, contests, book swaps—whatever we need to do, we should do it. Many of the teachers I know have two library cards: one for the town they live in and another for the town they teach in. Having both gives you even more access to books. If they know you're a teacher, they'll usually give you a higher allowance for the number of items you can check out.

It's powerful when you have books in multiple languages, and you can choose how you display them and "promote" them. I love having kids organize classroom libraries at the beginning of the year and again several times throughout the year because it gives them a taste of what's available for them to read. It also gives them a chance to read across genres and languages. As they grow in their reading skills and interests as the year progresses, they may have forgotten about the books they viewed once at the beginning of the year.

At the beginning of the year, we'd work to build up our collective reading stamina. I'd invite kids to disappear into their books, and they'd always ask me what I meant by that. I explained that when we are given time to read during school and anywhere else, we can disappear for a bit and be transported into whatever book we read. The kids would look around at each other, wondering if it was another one of my weird metaphors. I'd tell them that when we read together, we can almost get there, but when we read by ourselves or listen to an audiobook, things get magical!

After the first few times we'd set up for our independent reading, I'd ask kids where they went to and then it became a goal of theirs to disappear into those places, so they'd have something cool to share. This helped us in our writing later, because students were invited to share the sights, sounds, and smells of the places they visited: a classroom in the story, a mechanic's shop fixing up a Lamborghini, a soccer field with Lionel Messi, a character's home, etc. They became experts at incorporating sensory details into their writing.

Similar to launching a yoga or meditation session, I'd ask students to set their intentions for reading before we start. Sometimes, we're dying to find out what happens next. Other times, we're going to go back and reread a part that we didn't quite understand the first time around. Sometimes, we are just excited to start a new book or reread a favorite. Then, we'd begin. Kids could get themselves into whatever positions they wanted to be comfortable with. We worked on reading without getting distracted, and it was important for me to model that sometimes, I get distracted, too. If I have a list of things to do in my head, I may need to jot a few things down first before I can get comfortable reading.

After we'd sustain ourselves reading for a bit, I'd invite students to finish up their reading and find a good place to stop. For the first few minutes, I'd have students think about where they were. Then, I'd invite students to do a little bit of reflection——sometimes it is in a mini notebook, on a post-it, or creating a quick video entry about what they read. About once or twice each week, I'd invite students to talk to each other about their independent reading books.

Yes, I had kids do reading logs, and I modified them a lot because I couldn't quite get them to capture meaningful information. I wanted students to reflect across the week on the following things: what genres they read, what languages they chose to read in that week, what they were wondering about, and/or what surprised them. One of my favorite tools I developed was a bubble map for kids to fill in to help them keep track of the time spent reading in each language in our bilingual classroom. There was an English bubble and a Spanish bubble. Inside each were smaller bubbles, and kids were invited to shade in a bubble for each time they chose to read a book in that particular language. At the end of the week, students could see if they were reading across languages or sticking only to one language. It made for good reflections on how they were engaging with language and also gave me information, like the time when a student wrote that they wanted to read more in Spanish this week but the series she fell in love with was only available in our school library in English. *Good to know!* I made sure I added that series to our Spanish library a short time later.

MOVING BEYOND VIA REFLECTION & ACTION

Share out your reflections & action steps on Twitter using #MovingBeyondEdu

REFLECT:

- Which students, besides multilingual learners, benefit when you employ the above shifts and strategies?

ACT:

- What do you see as one transformational practice that you can try next week?

One practice I will try is...	I will try it (when/which content/class)...	My reflections after trying it are...

- How can you increase more opportunities for comprehensible input into your instruction?

One element of Comprehensible Input I will try to focus on is...	I will try it (when/which content/class)...	My reflections after trying it are...

BEYOND ONE LANGUAGE

ELEVATING & EMBRACING ALL OUR ASSETS

THE USE OF HOME LANGUAGE

*L*et's be real here for a moment. How many of you have a poster in your school that brags about how much you value your diversity? That's cool, I'm not hating on posters. I do wonder what pieces of evidence your school or district has in showing how much the system values its diversity. While this book focuses on our linguistic diversity, I'd love to expand here.

The political climate may not help students or their families feel that their linguistic diversity is celebrated. In Arizona, the public school system "banned" bilingual education and moved to provide "English-only" support. I wonder how the students and parents feel about moving from a model that allows students to access their full linguistic repertoire to only utilizing English? What language is welcome and which languages are no longer welcome? Through these policies, what parts of our students' identities are "unacceptable" in schools?

English-only policies are not based on research, best practice, or social-emotional development. They are based on fear, prejudice, and racism. If you look into the political campaigning done in Arizona, you will see that many of the English-only policies were funded by a man named Robert Unz, who is linked to anti-Semitism sentiments and white supremacy. But, I'll pause there because those folks don't belong in education, and they most certainly don't belong in this book.

What we can control is the culture we create in our classrooms and schools. Our kids deserve to come to classrooms that value their identities and honor their families' languages. Even more great news? We all can have an impact in doing this work—no matter our role, and no matter our linguistic skills!

OUR LINGUISTIC REPRESENTATION

If you've ever had the privilege of attending a professional learning opportunity from Karen Beeman and Cheryl Urow from Teaching For Biliteracy, you'll know how inspiring and knowledgeable they are. I've been lucky enough to work with them, read their book *Teaching for Biliteracy* (2012), and hear them both speak about elevating the status of other languages.

Because we are combating an "English-only" political climate outside the walls of the school, this makes it increasingly important that we actively seek to create an inclusive school community that values its linguistic diversity. One way to value the linguistic assets of your students is to look for ways to elevate the presence of our languages.

Want to dive in but afraid how to do this if you're monolingual? Fear not. You do not have to fake knowing a language to incorporate home languages into your instruction, conversation, assessment, or home communication. All it takes is an open mind and some humility.

One way to get a quick language inventory is to check in with your EL teacher, but I have a really fun and engaging alternative. An easy way that you can collect the languages is by having a class meeting (any grade level, any subject you teach, any group you serve). Grab your students all together and start a conversation about the languages that we have. Record them on a piece of paper or chart paper.

To illustrate how this may go, here's another dreamy classroom sequence. Ready?

Teacher: Languages are beautiful. They help us connect and communicate. They help us express our needs and help each other. We can communicate to show love, kindness, and express our feelings. Think to yourself of all the ways we communicate with our words.

Students: *thinking deeply*

Teacher: Now, I'd love to hear about all the beautiful languages that we have inside this very room. Right now, we're all using the English language, so I'll write that down here, off to the side. Besides English, what languages do you know that you use to communicate?

Students: *raise hands, share thoughts*

Teacher: Wow, how great is that!? Seven kids have shared so far- so let's add these languages to our paper. Isn't this incredible? Just think. If we were to connect with folks from our neighborhoods or travel to another town or state, or even another country- just think of how many people we can connect with through our languages!

Student A: You know, Mrs. Spina. I don't speak Korean, but my grandparents do. Does that count?

Teacher: YES! Of course—they are a part of our linguistic stories in this classroom because they are a part of your family. Let's add that to our list. Does someone else have a family that speaks another language?

Students: *more hands, more thoughts*

Teacher: Class, this is incredible. We now have 13 languages that are a part of our stories in this very classroom. How wonderful. Let's put this list on the door outside our room so that anyone who walks by can see how proud we are of our languages!

Students: *cheering* (confetti mysteriously falls from the ceiling)

End scene.

That, of course, was a high school example. Okay, I'm kidding. And, as a side note—if your confetti release machine in your classroom ceiling is broken, be sure you contact your building leadership ASAP.

We need to model conversations about how valuable our languages are to us, each other, and the world. It is also okay to admit if you are monolingual. The classroom dream sequence above gives us one way to have a conversation with our students about the languages of the classroom. I'm embedding one such recording tool here, and I'd encourage you to bring this to your team and your school. It's a great way for all of us to learn about our students' linguistic identities and hear about their linguistic stories.

The district I serve right now took on this opportunity with lots of support and energy. It was beautiful to me to walk down the hallways of our schools and see signs on many classroom doors/windows that proudly displayed their number of languages. Sometimes the kids wrote the languages, sometimes the teachers recorded it for them. Either way, it sent a powerful message to any visitors to our schools: *We are proud of our languages. Our languages are something to brag about. We are hanging this with pride for all to see.*

The next powerful moment that unfolds is when parents, guardians, and families come into the school for the next event. They walk down the hall, and something catches their eye. *Someone in room 106 speaks Lithuanian? I do, too... but I didn't teach my kids the language. I wonder if my son included our language on his classroom's poster?* Woah. This builds lots of great opportunities for deeper discussions at the family level.

This exercise could also bring about lots of powerful conversations about the pressure our families are given to learn English by a variety of sources, linguistic oppression in the US, language revitalization, language policies in different places, and language ideologies.

So, we know a little bit more about our languages—now what? What might be some of the ways we pull those into our instruction?

COGNATES

A cognate is a word that has the same linguistic derivation of another word—you have probably seen these before. Words like *fraction* in English and *fracción* in Spanish are an example of a pair of cognates. Do you see how similar they are? There are beautiful listings of cognates in many languages if you just do a few simple online searches. There is a lot of beauty, once again, in having students co-construct these listings as topics and units are studied. For example, during your geometry unit of 2D and 3D shapes, construct a few cognate lists and hang them up in the classroom. What's even cooler is to walk alongside students in analyzing the similarities and differences between the languages, which folks in the field refer to as "contrastive analysis." What language patterns are there? What remains the same and what is different?

FALSE COGNATES

When I was a student, I once tried to convince my entire high school Spanish class that I was so "embarazada" after tripping in the hallway before coming into class. If you are a Spanish speaker, you're either giggling or nodding in agreement, knowing my mistake. I was not *embarazada* at all, which my teacher hurriedly attempted to assure me and the class. However, I was confident that I was very much so. She finally asked me in English if I was pregnant. I was not. I was, however, tricked by a false cognate. If you have an additional language asset besides English, you can use your language superpowers to help students identify false cognates.

TRANSLANGUAGING

For multilingual students, it is important to keep in mind that they are not twice monolingual. This sounds silly, but many of us function this way in our understanding, especially if we are monolingual. I don't have a "Spanish brain" and an "English brain"; however, as an adult language learner, I do organize my language into spaces. There is an English space, a Spanish space, and a beautiful third linguistic space where the two languages interact, play tag and run around together. That third linguistic space is where I translanguage—I pull from my full linguistic repertoire. I even do this cool thing sometimes where I create words in my head by applying a Spanish rule to an English word, or vice versa. Developing in more than one language is not a clean process—words don't just gently float magically into the linguistic spaces in our minds. They plop into our repertoire, and the words need us to engage and play with them so that we can make sense of the words and their meanings, when to use them, and how to change or modify them in different contexts. As the educator, it is not my job to assign "correctness" or even labels to words that my students bring into the classroom. As Dr. José Medina always says, our job is to "validate and honor their words, and expand their linguistic repertoire!"

HOW ARE OUR LANGUAGES REPRESENTED ON THE WALLS OF THE SCHOOL?

We always have these great big posters in most schools that say, YAY DIVERSITY! or WE VALUE DIVERSITY! or something similar. Aside from that one poster, what other evidence is there on the walls of our schools that show that we value our linguistic diversity?

From the Blog: The Writing on the Wall

What's on the walls of our schools shows what the school values. If the school values their students' ideas, you will see samples of student work. If the school values a certain character education program, you will see evidence of this on the walls of the school and inside the classrooms. If the school values that their students hold themselves accountable to common expectations, this will also be evident by looking on the walls.

I understand that English is the language of instruction. It is our common language (or lingua franca, if you have studied EL curriculum & instruction!). There is nothing wrong with having these posters grace our walls. There is something wrong with publicly declaring that you value diversity without representing your linguistically diverse students and families.

This is truly an easy fix—but there are some Dos and Don'ts.

DO:
1. Walk around your school and see what you notice. Take a language inventory. Share with your school leadership team and suggest some changes. Most people are completely unaware of what their schools' appearance can share the school's values.
2. Gather data about your school's linguistically diverse population. Ask your administrator or EL teacher about

what language groups are in your school. Ask the students you serve questions about their linguistic assets.

3. Go on Amazon or your favorite retailer and search for signs and posters in other languages. Hang signs and posters *throughout* the school.

4. If you speak a language other than English, try to speak it in front of the students you serve. If several teachers speak a language other than English, try to use that language in social contexts (passing in the hallways, stopping for a quick conversation, etc.). When children see that teachers use a language other than English, especially for social conversations, the status of that language is instantly elevated.

5. As you get to know your students and their families, look for language liaisons in your classroom, school, or community. Check with your local community colleges, libraries, and public service agencies. These liaisons can help students to create posters, signs, ads for school events, school calendars, etc.

DON'T:

1. Don't cluster all of your linguistically diverse posters/signs in one spot (for example: on the wall outside of the EL classroom). This sends the message that this tiny corner of the school is the "Diversity Corner." Be sure that your artifacts are shared throughout the school so that it shows that this is a value everywhere- not just in one corner.

2. Don't make the signs look different based on the language. For example, if you have a professionally-made sign for the cafeteria, don't tape an index card underneath it with another language. Which language LOOKS more valuable to students and parents walking by? Also, be careful

not to always place the English sign on top of the other language. Again—which language LOOKS more valuable? If English is always on top, what message does that send?

3. Don't prohibit languages other than English to be used in classrooms, cafeterias, the bus, etc.. Not only is this a terrible sentiment, it is also quite illegal. It also breeds intolerance, fear, and a general disdain for linguistically diverse students and populations.

4. Don't assess this just once each school year. There should be an ongoing status-check of how a school is doing in its effort to elevate the status of other languages. Perhaps one member of the school's leadership team can be charged with reporting to the team each month and sharing with the rest of the building. What are our celebrations? Which teachers have shown great examples of elevating other languages this month?

NOTE: Don't make this the job of the EL teacher. ALL ADULTS in the building should care about lifting up ALL STUDENTS.

5. Don't force this by creating inauthentic examples of language elevation. See how your teachers can infuse their instruction with linguistic opportunities, such as through a cognate wall, etc. Infuse your vocabulary posters with other languages. Walking around the school and seeing the word "turtle" in other languages feels random and is not connected to any learning.

What are your favorite ways to elevate the status of other languages in your building? What are on your list of Dos and Don'ts? What are some things that you have tried that you'd encourage others to try?

LINGUISTIC REPRESENTATION ASSESSMENT TOOL

 It may be helpful for school leadership teams, or even student leadership teams, to walk the halls of the school and take a quick inventory of how the school is doing. I'm going to share one such tool in the QR code for monitoring your linguistic representation across your school. This is a very basic starting point, so you can feel free to use this tool or create your own tool that assesses how your learning community is representing the linguistic diversity that you're so proud of in your school!

LINGUISTIC ISLANDS

A comment we all hear a lot but we don't unpack often is this: "*But they were born here.*" Notice this phrase is different from "*They were born here.*"

This comment makes me cringe because it's full of expectations and assumptions. When I speak about this at conferences, the crowd of EL teachers usually nods right along with me. Lots of folks have heard this very phrase uttered in their schools, usually around the problem-solving table.

But they were born here.

The phrase often follows a comment like, "This student is still acquiring the academic language of social studies" or "This student has been in an EL program for four years."

But they were born here.

Ugh. Let's start unpacking.

For whatever reason, it is more concrete for adults to understand when a student is coming to the US from another country and is acquiring the English language. It seems that more allowances are made for them and adults are more flexible to meet their needs. When adults around the table learn that the student was born in the US and is enrolled in an EL program or is identified as an EL student, the adults who serve them are less likely to view them as an EL, in need of scaffolds and support.

You may be surprised to learn that most students who are identified as English Learners are born in the US. There's a strange assumption though, that being born in the US gives students this natural ability to speak, listen, read, and write in English. It's as if folks believe that something magical happens in utero or perhaps it happens through the birth process in an American hospital that grants babies this English-language mastery.

It doesn't.

Our multilingual learners grow up with access to the languages of their families—which are all beautiful, important, and part of their identities. There are families in our neighborhoods who speak their heritage language all day and all night; it is the language of the home, their house of faith, the grocery stores they frequent, and more. Many call this idea a "linguistic island." When students arrive at school, they can continue their language development, which may sometimes mean *beginning* their English language development.

MOVING BEYOND VIA REFLECTION & ACTION

Share out your reflections & action steps on Twitter using #MovingBeyondEdu
REFLECT:

- Even if you are a monolingual educator, how do you intentionally and purposefully express appreciation and respect for languages other than English?
- Have you witnessed linguistic oppression in your community? Have you observed linguistically oppressive conversations online? How can you use your role as a change agent to disrupt these situations?

ACT:

- Make a list: What are your schools' top languages represented by students, families, and staff?

Our top languages are...

1.	
2.	
3.	
4.	
5.	

*Complete a Language Inventory of your classroom or learning space. Make an action plan based on what you've noticed. An example tool is linked below.

*Complete a Language Inventory of your school and assess what's on your walls. What does it show and tell about your school values? An example tool is linked below.

BEYOND SEL

EDUCATOR MINDSETS, SHIFTS, & MOVES

WHERE THE WORK STARTS

We have a large number of folks in the US who are completely and utterly *offended* over pushing the one button for English on robocalls. "We live in the US. We should all speak English."

Our students are growing up in this environment of linguistic and cultural oppression. Where's the part of the math curriculum that addresses what to do when a group of students is harassed by another group of students on the playground chanting anti-immigrant rhetoric?

When our students don't see themselves in our curriculum, it's as if they don't exist: their histories, their stories, their perspectives are not represented or shared. Even worse, when our students see themselves in our curriculum, but they are misrepresented: their stories are white-washed and colonialized, and this is highly problematic.

We can't talk about social-emotional support for multilingual learners without first addressing anti-immigrant rhetoric, institutionalized racism, linguistic oppression, white privilege, and unconscious bias. That's where we need to start.

The work needs to start with each of us as individuals. It is life work, not weekend work. It is a lifelong journey, not a webinar or a training. It is a commitment to continuous growth (and yes, lots of mess-ups along the way, too) and reflection. The work starts there.

I will also note that it is important for educators to be trauma-informed. This is also a journey of understanding and intentional practice at improving our routines, structures, and systems

RESPECTING & PROTECTING STUDENTS' STORIES

This section is not where I go into sad, happy, devastating, shocking, triumphant, or heartbreaking stories about my kids.

All of the students that I have served for the last 15 years have their own stories. I know snippets of them. Many have trusted me with them. Many have opened up to me, and many have not. Given my role serving linguistically diverse communities, the students I serve are first-generation, second-generation (and beyond) immigrants—and their paths are varied and beautiful, but they belong to them.

It is not my right to tell their stories. Those are not my stories to tell. I'm not going to tell their stories but use pseudonyms. Whenever my students grow up, they can choose whether or not to tell their stories, and I'll support them 100% if and when they do or don't.

I will tell some of the stories about the magic of our classroom —because those were the stories we shared and built together. Our classroom was magical because of the students I served, not because of me. I share these stories in hopes that you can use the magic of your students to create experiences that celebrate all the amazingness that they bring into your classroom.

I'm also not going to paint a picture of my students that misrepresents them. We can look up all the statistics about multi-lingual learners if that's what we want; however, we have to remember that the student group with an EL-identifier is not homogenous. They all have different experiences in life, just like monolingual students. I'm not going to say that all my students were living in poverty, suffered from childhood traumas, had a single parent raising them, or whatever else folks want to assume about my kids. I don't wish to feed into anyone's narratives about the kids I serve.

ARE WE "ASSESSING" THEIR STORIES?

Our students' privacy is important. It is a privilege to serve our students, but *it is not our right to know their stories.* Don't make kids tell their arrival stories (or those of their families) for academic points. Don't make them relive any traumas for the sake of a presentation or an essay. While some stories are triumphant, others may be tragic. We cannot invade the privacy of their families for a grade or rate their experiences on a rubric. We can work continu-ously to create spaces for them that feel safe to share their thoughts and feelings, if they so choose. We can work continuously to build community learning spaces that are based on trust and empathy. The bottom line is that we must respect our students, their fami-lies, and their privacy. If a student feels inclined to share, let them call the shots and determine their purpose, their product, and their audience. Their experience and story should never be up for debate or ever necessitate any "feedback" from you unless you are thanking them for choosing to share.

SAYING OUR STUDENTS' NAMES CORRECTLY

This one may seem obvious, but we need to take the time to learn how to pronounce our students' names correctly.

From the Blog: I Value Your Name, Teach Me How to Say it Correctly!

Our names are a large part of our identity. As we welcome new students to a new school year, we want to be sure that we are honoring each student's identity by saying their names correctly!

Our students should feel empowered and respected while they are at school. If we take the time to learn, it sets a tone of mutual respect. After hearing educator, speaker, equity leader, and author Huda Essa speak about her book, Teach Us Your Name, I thought that the FlipGrid platform (or Seesaw, or something else similar!) would be a great way for students to leave a quick video teaching us how to say their names!

Check out her Ted Talk here, called Your Name is the Key! Her video (accessible in the QR Code on the next page) is wonderful, and it would be great to share it with your staff! If you can ever hear her speak, be sure to attend. She's wonderful!

Please note...

*This can be used in every classroom at every level.

*This should never be used on only a select group of students (for example—do not just have your linguistically diverse students complete this task and no one else). I'd suggest an entire class doing this—yes, even students named Elizabeth and John can teach how to say their name, even if in a given school these are common names.

*This is helpful for students, teachers, substitute teachers, principals, custodians, coaches, educational associates, interventionists, nurses, etc!

*There are different settings within FlipGrid so you can adjust who you want to be able to access the video thread/topic. Please check with your district's tech policies!

*Utilizing platforms like these are also a great way to introduce digital citizenship and practice oral language skills.

In addition to Huda Essa's work mentioned in the blog, other wonderful children's books to explore (and to read aloud to your staff at a staff meeting—seriously, do it):

Alma and How She Got Her Name by Juana Martinez-Nael
The Name Jar by Yangsook Choi
Hope by Isabell Monk
Thunder Boy, Jr by Sherman Alexie
Your Name is a Song by Jamilah Thompkins-Bigelow

You may note that some kids will give themselves nicknames to make it *easier for you* to say their name. It is so important that we take the time to learn how to pronounce our students' names. Our names are a part of our histories, our stories, our cultures, our families. They matter. They are valuable.

If kids can learn all of our names as teachers, you can learn to say students' names in a way that shows respect to them. Take the time needed.

AUTHENTIC REPRESENTATION MATTERS

When our students don't see themselves in our curriculum, it's as if they don't exist: their histories, their stories, their perspectives. Even worse—when our students see themselves in our curriculum, but the stories are not accurate, misrepresented, or told by someone who truly has no business telling the story from "their" respective.

When narratives are being told about the students we serve (by the media, by the government, by their social media feeds, by celebrities, by Hollywood, by our social studies textbooks, or even by other educators, etc.), we need to give them the space to address it, process it, beat it up, and do something with it.

Let me be clear—we don't need to *give them* a voice. They already have a voice. They already have the thoughts, the words, the sentences, the speeches, the novels, the dissertations. They don't need a voice. They need the platform, confidence, and tools to use it. It is our job to ensure their voices along with their stories, experiences, and histories are not only heard but sought out.

FOOD INSECURITY

Throughout my years in the classroom, I tried to work with my students to support whatever struggles they were having, whether they were academic or not. One battle that seemed to strike more than once was food insecurity.

Food insecurity is a term that is used to describe the situation in which one does not have consistent and reliable access to food. This does not necessarily mean that everyone who qualifies for free/reduced meals is also food insecure. It also does not mean that those who don't qualify for free breakfast are necessarily food-secure. Food insecurity can last a long time, or it could be limited to a short season of life. This happens to families across the US, regardless of their race, ethnicity, language, and socioeconomic class.

Our schools' food policies are created to keep children safe at school. There are so many allergies, and educators must be aware of allergens that are in many of our food products. Most allergies are known, but not always.

We need to be responsive to our students' physical needs—that may mean looking for ways to implement a healthy snack option for those who do not have the means to bring a snack. For some students, that may mean looking at meal distributions via back-packs for weekends and breaks from school.

For other students, they may have a more complicated relationship with food insecurity. There may be a student or two that has severe anxiety related to food, even birthday treats. For some, if they heard there was a birthday treat being distributed that afternoon, it might set them off. There have been students over the years who needed to walk down to the front office to view the treats, and physically place a post-it with their name on it on one of the items. Others needed to bring it into the classroom and store it on their desk until it was time to eat.

For some students, it made sense for them to take a break every day at a certain time to read a book and have a snack. For others, it made sense for them to have unlimited access to snacks—99% of the time, it was not abused.

When you have students who are battling food insecurity, it is important to have a team behind you and seek out the expertise of your school social worker, nurse, nutritionist, and parents. We'll explore this more later when we talk about community connections.

WHEN THEY'RE TIRED

If students are hungry, get them food. When our students need rest, we need to let them rest. Have you ever been told to make tired kids stand so that they don't fall asleep? That seems abusive. I know I can't work well or concentrate when I'm exhausted. I need my sleep! And of course, everyone's sleep patterns and preferences are different. For me, I feel dysregulated when I didn't sleep well the night before. Like you, I have had students over the years who would come to class utterly exhausted (that went beyond morning grogginess). Their exhaustion led to dysregulation. So after some brainstorming, we found a spot in the school that they could rest when they needed to, have a healthy snack if needed, and then return to class. Sometimes the students would request to stay in our classroom and put their heads down on their desks, and I would let them. Sometimes a teacher would come in with an announcement for the class, or an administrator would come in for a visit and look at me quizzically, but I'd just let them know that the student is resting, and we'd leave it at that.

It is so important that we communicate our students' needs to the other adults in the building. We don't have to share their stories necessarily, but we do need to share the needs. Many times, our colleagues and teammates could offer us ideas or be great thought partners for us, but other times, it's just helpful to be informed.

For some students, the exhaustion is because of a season of difficulty at home. For others, staying up late means they can enjoy the only time they have with a working parent during the week. Other times, the student may be kept up late due to a noisy sibling, a loud neighbor—or other things like fear, anxiety, sleep disorders, etc. And sure, sometimes, kids are tired because they're up late playing video games.

We can inform the families of what we notice without accusing them of having an unfit household. We can help families understand how tired the student is at school, and we can come up with a plan to help the student be successful at school. Involving families is critical. That's *their* child!

LUNCH WITH THE TEACHER

Another great teacher move for us to consider is our incentive systems. We always talk about the need to develop intrinsically-motivated students but then we keep prize boxes in our classrooms or front offices. I was at a conference once, and the presenter asked how many of us ate lunch with our students. Most hands went up. The presenter then asked how many of us ate lunch with our students as a reward? About half of the hands went up. She pushed our thinking forward.

Since then, I've thought about that—how many of us are using

Lunch with the Teacher as a reward? Is it such a gift for our kids to be able to spend time with us, or should we just choose to do that (if we desired) because we love our kids and enjoy being with them?

"THANKS FOR BEING SO QUIET."

Another teacher move to consider is our language choices when we praise students. It is wise for all of us to teach our students to be respectful members of our school community. Many schools have some type of expectation for noise levels in the hallways, but I had to check my language. It hit me like a ton of bricks one night (you know—that time of your day when you lie in bed but instead of sleeping you run through your entire day, worry about Clara's test, beat yourself up over the lesson that flopped, make mental to-do lists, and obsess over that argument you got into seven years ago).

After attending a few rounds of training for Safe & Civil Schools work as well as reading *Teach Like a Champion*, I became hyper-aware of the words that I said to my students, especially in terms of laying out expectations for behaviors.

Something I always said to my class while we walked through the hallways was, "I love how you're being so quiet," or "Thanks for being so quiet." I almost always said that, and I thought it was *just wonderful* that I was giving my students positive praise. But that night in bed, I thought deeper about it. When using those words, what exactly was I praising?

What I meant to praise was their respect for others, but instead, I was praising their silence. As an educator of a group of students that our systems have tried to silence for generations, I had to check myself and reflect on my language choices. If I wanted to praise their respect, then those were the words I needed to say. *Thank you for being respectful of other people's learning* would be most appropriate here.

Instead of saying "I love how you _____," I needed to remove myself from the equation. I don't want any students behaving a certain way to please me. I don't hold any power over my students. I wanted my students to feel empowered to make decisions that they thought were best. I made a conscious effort to monitor my language.

POWER STRUGGLES

We can be reflexive as educators about the moments where we may find ourselves engaging in power struggles with students. I've caught myself several times! We can't engage in power struggles with students, period. It just doesn't work, and no one wins. An escalated adult can't de-escalate anyone else. There are moments in class where teachers have gotten angry or frustrated, or have even lost our cool. It is critical for us to be mindful of what raising our voice one time can do to destroy relationships we have built over time.

The work we do is hard. It's exhausting. When we feel burned out or like we're not trusted by our leadership, it's hard. When we get another email that adds five more things to our to-do list, it feels deflating. We have bad days. Not every day in the classroom is a good day. Let's be real. We are humans with feelings. We make mistakes. We are not perfect. We can love our jobs and our students but also recognize that some days just don't feel good.

No matter what, our kids deserve respect, just like we do. If our students don't feel like we will treat them with kindness and compassion even on the hard days, or even when they're pushing our buttons, then we have some work to do.

When we have moments of escalation in our classrooms, it is very easy for us to become escalated.

Allow yourself the moments to practice a pause. Excuse yourself from conversations when you feel like you're starting to lose it —and also, equip students with the tools for them to self-advocate and excuse themselves from having conversations with you when they're escalated. We have to do whatever we can to stay calm, even when it's hard. We can't resort to shaming or humiliating our students. Give yourself and the student a chance to say, "I need a little bit of time. Let's talk about this when we both feel calmer." It's a good skill to model and it can also save the relationship you have with the students you serve.

MOVING BEYOND VIA REFLECTION & ACTION

Share out your reflections & action steps on Twitter using #MovingBeyondEdu

REFLECT:

- How do you support students who are battling food insecurity? How does your school?
- What practices do you have in place to support students who are exhausted?

ACT:

- How do you ensure that you are pronouncing students' names correctly? Make a plan and identify tools you may use to help you and your colleagues in this work.

How do I learn how to say each student's name? List out tools or steps below:	At the beginning of the year or semester..	Periodically Revisiting throughout the year/semester...
1,		
2.		
3.		

- How do you model respect for students when you ask students to correct you until you have it right?

"It's important that I say your name correctly."	"Will you please correct me? It's important to me."
"Thank you for helping me pronounce your name. It's important that I keep practicing it."	"Your name is beautiful. Please teach me to say it."

- What do you do if you find yourself becoming escalated while with a student?

Be mindful of your body and your mind. I know I'm feeling escalated when...	*Be aware of moments to stop, pause, regroup, or reframe.* When I feel escalated, I will need to...
1.	1.
2.	2.
3.	3.

6

BEYOND INSPIRATION

PRACTICES THAT EMPOWER

*I*n this section, it is my hope to share different strategies and activities that you may wish to try out in your space, or take as an idea and put your own twist on it! As I continue to grow, I always reflect back and refine my practice.

HOW WE ADDRESS OUR STUDENTS

What do you call your students when you talk to them? Do you call them kids? Scholars? Here are some thoughts and considerations for us.

Instead of: Gendered terms (Boys and Girls, Ladies and Gentlemen, etc.) that aren't very inclusive, you can try some of these: *Class, Students, Scholars, Writers, Mathematicians, Future World Leaders, Future CEOs, Business Partners, Brilliant Minds, Marvelous Multilingual Experts, Future Presidents, Professionals, Colleagues, Friends, Scientists, Inspiration Seekers, Risk Takers,* etc. How could those small moments build our students up over time?

I asked students in my 3rd grade class how they wanted me to refer to them. One year, they preferred to be called "Los Patitos" (*ducklings*). Another year, they wanted to be called "Los Presidentes" because they all wanted to be future presidents of their companies, businesses, or country! Sometimes, students asked me to call them different things, like during our science class. More on that later!

THE COLLEGE PROJECT

There was a project I began with tons of excitement, but I got it wrong at first. Like, really wrong.

I am a proud first-generation college student, but I have found myself out of my element a time or two. Once I was in a meeting full of privileged folks who sat around the table sharing where their parents attended college, and several even shared how many buildings on campus were named after their family members. Sheesh. The conversation eventually turned to me, and I was asked a question that emerged out of an assumed privilege that stopped me dead in my tracks: "Carly, where did your parents go to college?"

The third graders I served spoke a lot like me. Through conversations, we found that our parents had the same dreams for us: to go to college. "Maestra, mi mamá me dice que un día voy a la universidad. One day I'm going to college. So I have to work hard now to set me up for college." Yes, my parents had the same dream for me and my sisters, and they talked about it a lot: *Work hard, get good grades, you'll have to put this on your college application.*

Over the years, I had a vision of starting a fun project, so one year, we finally went for it. We wrote snail mail to colleges and universities across the country, and we asked them to send our class a bumper sticker. We wanted to make a College Wall in our classroom and line the ceiling tiles with bumper stickers. The hope was that it would function as a sort of Vision Board. We asked for bumper stickers because we figured they'd be small, cheap, and easy to ship. We also noted in our letters that if they couldn't send a bumper sticker, we'd love a pamphlet about their university so we could learn about their programs.

We were excited when we got our first envelope. We hung it proudly on an empty wall that we reserved for our College Wall. We did a quick Google search and found out where the university was, what their most popular programs were, and what athletics programs that students could participate in.

That first envelope got us all excited. Someone read our letter. Someone wanted us to know about their college. Someone wanted us to *attend* their college.

Then weeks went by without any other response. So we sent out a few more batches of snail mail and expanded our reach. Then, we waited.

The project blew up. We hardly got any bumper stickers.

...Instead, *boxes* started to roll in. Giant, stuffed envelopes would clog my teacher inbox in the staff room. My amazing administrative assistant (who was the Queen of the School, I tell you—our schools' office staff never get the credit they deserve) would celebrate each package with me, ask me which schools were recruiting my future college students, and even sometimes drop off packages to our classroom herself. Colleges sent us boxes full of pamphlets, pencils, posters, maps, pictures, postcards, keychains, logos, and tons of other promotional items. A few of the bigger schools even sent *a t-shirt for every child in my classroom*. Wow, did we celebrate receiving those shirts! We were all jumping up and down, and we threw those shirts on right over our outfits. We took about a million selfies posing in our shirts. I cannot tell you how much we strutted around the school on those days. We were on Cloud Nine! As we saw it, we were practically all Clemson-bound.

Our college board filled up—and fast. We quickly had to create additional spaces around our classroom, in the hallway and even borrowed our colleagues' hallway bulletin boards. We draped pennants from our ceiling tiles (which I can most certainly say violated fire code—yikes!).

We were filled up! We thought we were the coolest kids in school. In a lot of ways, we were. My students would tell me which college football games they watched on the weekends. They'd make it a point to ask the other teachers in the school which colleges they attended (we even graphed it by each state during our math unit on data collection). The class would find different university names in our science articles. We made list after list of colleges and universities that we heard from. We felt inspired by each piece of mail we received.

We took to social media and learned how to Tweet and make posts on Instagram and tag the schools to thank them for sending us mail. We'd get tagged in posts and squeal with excitement. Then we'd check out the social media feeds of their school and sports teams and departments.

The kids started to wonder how many states we had represented in our listing of schools, so we started to track it. Each student had their own copy of the map and we colored in all the states we had so far—and they started to learn the geography of the US. Oh, California? *Hey, that's pretty close to our friends in Nevada.* I realized how much the learning was "sticking" when weeks later, in the middle of Reading, the students started to panic. We were analyzing a nonfiction text related to a current event: a tornado touched down in Oklahoma, and the text was sharing details about the damage. I was so confused with all the screams and shouts, I almost got frustrated with the kids. I asked what they were so upset about. "*Our friends*, Mrs. Spina! Are they okay? Can you call them? Can we send them a message?"

Our friends. They were concerned about our friends at Oklahoma State University, who sent us a fun package just weeks earlier. My heart overflowed and I stopped the lesson. We went and peeked online to do some research and we learned that the tornado was not near the university, or anywhere near other Oklahoma schools that were our friends.

When the class felt that connected to a university far away in another state, I felt like we were doing something good. My kids had empathy that was off the charts to begin with, but they inspired me so much.

Throughout the project, throughout the year, we learned a lot. We learned about how addresses worked and where to place them on an envelope. We learned about the postal service, stamps, and postage costs as we wrote down all the postage totals—*How much did that package cost to send us?*—and we were able to use that data in math class when we learned about adding decimals, rounding, graphing, and more. We learned about school departments and programs. We learned how to write a friendly letter, how to interact with universities on social media, and how to navigate college websites. We learned abbreviations for the states and where they all were located on a map. We learned about time zones and how to formulate opinions based on research. We learned about gratitude and how to write a meaningful thank you letter. We had the best time!

WHAT I GOT WRONG & HOW I CHANGED IT

I did get some things wrong with this study, and I made some changes. My biggest change: while encouraging a college-going culture was great, I needed to emphasize that *going to college isn't the end-all-be-all indicator of success.* It just isn't. My students' parents and my parents didn't go to college and *they were still all success stories*. Did our parents struggle sometimes? Sure, but I think all parents do at some point, regardless of whether or not they attended a university. Let's not limit our ideas of what success looks like. I shouldn't be telling kids (or myself) that the only way to be successful is to go to college. So in the years to follow, we changed it up. We spread our scope outward so it became more about lifelong learning. We wrote to trade schools, beauty schools, community colleges, apprenticeship programs, online schools, military groups—you name it, we researched it. We had endless options and inspiration to keep growing... and after all this effort in lifelong learning, new passions and interests emerged. This got us all thinking—wow, there are lots of careers out there, huh?

BUSINESS CARDS

Well, you can guess what happened next. After studying all of these programs out there across the US and beyond, we started learning about all these crazy careers we had never even heard of, and we needed to know more. It amazed us that new careers are popping up all the time. A social media manager? That job didn't exist a few years ago! A new idea was born moments after I showed them my husband's business card, after talking about what an engineer does. The kids were amazed over the idea of business cards, and we decided we needed some more.

We talked about the purpose of the card. It was a professional and confident way to introduce yourself to others. It gives folks a little taste of what you do and what your job is, and it lets people know how to contact you. Our favorite business cards were the ones that listed how many languages the professional spoke. We found that very important and *very impressive.*

We started collecting business cards. I put a few posts on my personal Facebook account, and the response was huge. We had a shopping bag full of about 800 or so business cards. We did so much with them! We sorted them by career type (STEM careers were the house favorite). We analyzed the information on each card as a way to represent the person, the company, and the career. A few students realized they had a passion for graphic design, and they wanted to make their own business cards... and so... another idea was born.

RESUMÉS

As the students started to dream big about what types of careers they wanted to have after going to their continued learning institution of choice, they asked if every job gives you a little business card. We talked about resumés. I showed them mine and asked them for their feedback—would they hire me if they were in charge? A few said yes, but others took me by the hand and shook their head sadly. I loved that honesty! The overwhelming sense was that I didn't show enough of my personality and it felt like a boring list. I asked them what they thought a resumé should have, and they had some great ideas.

They started to write their own resumes, listing out all the skills and talents they have, including their language skills. I asked them what they thought they'd add to it as the years went by. We shared some thoughts. Then one day, I had a student put a note on my desk. It was folded up and had some tears in it from where things were erased. What I read on the paper blew my mind. He had spent two hours the night before dreaming up big, beautiful dreams (that I know he's going to accomplish, no doubt in my mind) and listed out all of his *future accomplishments*. He wrote what schools he attended and what he studied at each one. He listed out fun things he accomplished as well, like skydiving and playing professional soccer for three years—unfortunately, he "had to stop because of a knee injury when he was 23". Yes, he was *that* specific.

Other students felt inspired to write their own resumes. They also asked me to do my future resume, so as a lifelong learner with lots left to accomplish and dream in life, I agreed. We all shared our future resumes and updated our business cards, which we swapped like baseball cards.

We talked about job interviews and ways to present ourselves to be professional but also be ourselves. "Like, Mrs. Spina, you're a professional teacher, but you still wear pink all the time, right? Or like how you make faces in all the pictures you take, but you can give a speech very calmly?" Yep, just like that.

One day, we did a mock-interview. One of my young ladies wanted the challenge of interviewing me for a job as a marine biologist. We set up two seats at the front of the room: one for her, one for me. The rest of the class sat around us, ready to give me feedback on my professionalism. My sweet class of third graders even whispered wishes of good luck and gave me many thumbs-up gestures as I modeled taking a big breath before walking towards my potential future boss. I pulled out my hand to offer a handshake, and she giggled, took my hand, and squeezed my index finger. Boom—another idea.

BUSINESS PARTNERS

My future professionals were accustomed to dreaming now, and they inspired me constantly. I think we all dream of all the ways that our students will grow up and become these amazing leaders and human beings—as parents, as professionals, as passion-seekers, as friends, and as community members. I thought they needed one more skill for their professional toolbelt: a strong handshake.

Now, we spent a lot of time before this lesson talking about customs, traditions, cultures, etc. We knew that in some cultures, only men shook hands. In some cultures, you only used your right hand and in others, you used your left. In some cultures, you didn't touch someone's hands at all—ever—unless they were married to you or a member of your family.

I asked in my parent newsletter if everyone would be okay learning about handshakes and they all thought it sounded like fun, so I continued.

I shared the story of how my sweet, southern grandpa would judge a man by the quality of his handshake. That's how I knew he approved of my husband (back when we were teenagers) because he commented on what a firm handshake he had. My students giggled with laughter, and then we practiced handshakes that were strong and showed the other person that we were confident and meant business. Soon, handshakes started popping up when the "scientists" entered the "laboratory" during science class. Handshakes became the way we greeted each other.

BUSINESS MEETINGS

As our learning continued, my class realized that we could spruce up our times meeting in partners, whether we were reading, working on a social studies project, or discussing math problems. Whenever we had partner tasks, we opted to call them Business Partners and we began and ended each "meeting" with a strong handshake. We introduced greetings like, "It's so great to see you today, Karla" and ended meetings with, "I'm proud of the work you did today, Alondra. Hope to see you soon." Group work switched from being called "groups" to "colleagues." The kids were all business, all the time and they kept me on my A-game.

CAREER FAIR

The students wanted to share their learning and ramp it up on a notch, so they asked if they could share it with more folks. We had a parent workshop night coming up, so I asked my principal if my kids could lead it with a career fair. He said yes. We got a bunch of used tri-fold boards and covered them with construction paper for a fresh background. The kids wrote letters to local professionals (they got to choose who we invited and which careers were showcased), and then they got to work creating a trifold board telling everyone what the career was. They had the chance to do some independent research, wrote emails with interview questions, printed pictures, and our classroom graphic designers were on call to offer insight about the ways to best represent their classmates' content on their board. The students designed a chart with possible interview questions for other kids to walk around and use with a clipboard and talk to the professional who would stand at the student-created board that showed their career. The night of the event rolled around, and we filled up our entire cafeteria with professionals of all types: pharmacists, police officers, engineers, graphic designers, small business owners, a pediatrician, and many others. The students chose the careers they wanted at the fair but also created a listing of other careers that they were interested in around the room. I watched in awe as my young professionals shook hands with the professionals around the room and asked them questions, carefully weighing their responses to shape their dreams.

MANTRA

One of our social-emotional learning lessons in the district-approved program was about positive self-talk. The students laughed out loud at the part of the lesson where I talked to myself, modeling positive self-talk before taking a test. "You're even more nuts than we thought, Mrs. Spina—you talk to yourself," they laughed. I told them that I talk to myself all the time, especially in moments of trouble, or when I accomplish a goal. Once we talked through a few more examples, they admitted that they also have thoughts that they use to motivate themselves, especially when they're trying to behave at home and not fight with their siblings! Growing up with two sisters and a mama with a watchful eye, I can relate! Some finally admitted that yes, they have talked to themselves before, and they've also heard family members, teachers, classmates, and even characters on TV shows do the same thing.

After some rich discussion, we made a list of some positive self-talk examples and moments when they'd use them. For example, before taking a test, a student may say to themselves, "I can do this!" Or before taking that free throw while playing basketball during their physical education class, one may say to themselves, "Follow through with your fingers, I got this!" We talked through a few more examples.

I'll never forget how one scholar shyly raised his hand. Usually, he didn't participate much during discussions with his voice, but he always participated with his listening. He asked, "Are we only supposed to do this when stuff is hard? Or can we do it when stuff is good, too? Or if we're bored?"

Woah. What a powerful and deeply reflective question from this student. I thanked him for his beautiful questions and I turned it over to the class, "What do you all think?"

The kids were eager to share, and all seemed to agree that positive self-talk works well when the good stuff is happening, too:

"If we got a good grade on a project, we can tell ourselves that we did a great job!"

"If I did a bunch of chores at home for my mom, I would tell myself that I helped her a lot and I'm very helpful."

I turned them back to the other question: What if we're bored? Silence. This one was a bit trickier. I reiterated that we all felt confident that positive self-talk was good for the good times and the hard times. Someone asked, "What would we even say to ourselves when nothing's happening?"

I'm telling you, children are brilliant questioners.

I asked them what messages would always be good for them to hear. We reflected. We journaled. A week later, our classroom mantra was born. We worked through a few drafts together, but we landed in a place that we all loved.

I believe in myself. I can do hard things. I can work really hard. I keep going when things get tough. I can get help when I need it. My teachers believe in me. They love me and care about me. I am important. I am loved. I will do amazing things.

These are the things I want for my students (past and future) and my children to always know and believe about themselves. I want all my nieces and nephews to believe these words. I even want these beliefs to be ingrained into my own heart for myself.

When I asked the kids what we should do with our mantra now that it was complete, at first we all kind of shrugged. We looked at it, proud of it, hanging on the poster. It felt anti-climactic, almost as if all that work was for nothing. I wanted to hop in and offer suggestions, but I knew I needed to wait it out. They needed to own this.

After a few (very long) minutes, some of the students started to offer ideas—during a math test, before a soccer game, when you get bad news, etc. Then one student stated that those were still all good things or bad things.

Finally, one scholar said we should say it in the morning when we wake up or while we brush our teeth because it would be a strong way to start the day! The class agreed with her. Another student said that he might say it at the end of the day after he prays with his family. Everyone thought that was a good idea, too. After further discussion, it was decided that everyone would get a copy of our mantra to hang up at home and say when they felt it was best. We also agreed that we should say it, loud and proud, all together at the beginning of the school day.

We started the next day. We said it every single day, and soon we all had it memorized. One day, a student asked if we could say it after lunch and recess because it would help her refocus after playing. Then we all started to say it twice a day. There were certain days around a presidential election where we started to say it before we left for the school day because we found that it gave us comfort when we were feeling anxious.

Kids would write our mantra in their journals, on their folders, or in notes to each other. Those words were tacked to our ceiling tiles so we could always see them and they were printed on our business cards we gave to each other. The words became our bookmarks and our favorite thing to post on social media. Those words wound up on small pieces of paper fixed to our desks with contact paper.

When I moved into a different role in the school district years later, I had former students drop by my office in the middle school and leave a wadded up piece of paper on my desk. Written out word-for-word was our classroom mantra from years ago. I still don't know which student threw it on my desk, but when I read it by myself, I was overwhelmed by emotion. I smoothed out the paper and taped it to my wall as a tear rolled down my cheek.

INSPIRATION WALLS

One of my favorite things to do as a young teen (and okay, maybe as an adult, too) was to grab a bunch of magazines and chop them up to make collages. I'd take my favorite words, my favorite fashion looks, quotes, scenes of tropical destinations, and pretty nail polish colors. I felt like a Teen Vogue editor, and the whole thing brought me joy.

We can find joy and inspiration all around us if we actively look for it. We were reading a poem once that we loved, and the kids asked if we could hang it up in our room. I told them to choose a spot. They picked our whiteboard and hung it with a magnet. A few days later, someone brought in a picture of their uncle who had just passed away and asked if they could hang it up, too. Naturally, as the days went by, more and more kids asked for space to hang something of importance to them. So we decided that we needed a dedicated space for this in the classroom. They elected a spot on our wall, away from the whiteboard, and closer to a little nook with an ottoman and pillows. It became our Inspiration Wall.

While we read, learned, explored, and connected in our classroom, we each picked and chose things that we thought were sources of inspiration, and we added those things to our spaces.

One Monday morning, one of my students burst into the door of the classroom holding up her district-issued iPad. "Maestra, maestra, mire!" she called. "*Look!*" She was so excited to share that she had spent this weekend creating her own Inspiration Wall. It was beautiful. Her mother wrote her a short note for the wall. Her little sister drew her a picture to hang up. She hung up a few college brochures from our college mail. She also hung up a few assignments that she was proud of. It was beautiful!

Many of the kids asked if they could create Inspiration Walls at home. I told my student that she inspired more inspiration! She beamed. I told the class that they'd have to talk to their parents about it, but I would write their families a letter to talk about what we thought about our classroom Inspiration Wall. We agreed that it probably wasn't a good idea to tape anything to our walls at home, especially if anyone's landlords asked our parents not to use tape! We discussed a few alternatives to having an Inspiration Wall: an inspiration notebook, a virtual inspiration wall on our iPads, and an inspiration playlist of songs.

CLASSROOM DESIGN THAT EMPOWERS

In just the same way that I work and continue to grow in the way I represent the languages of our school, I also want to treat the flags of my students with just as much respect as the US flag (as an educator in the US). While the majority of the students I serve were of Mexican descent, there were many other countries represented as well: Guatemala, Ecuador, El Salvador, and Cuba, just to name a few. It's important that I displayed their flags with equal care and attention as the US flag. To be more specific, I didn't have a large US flag and teeny, tiny flags representing other countries. All the flags were held at equal height and all flags were the same size.

One professional passion that unfolded as I was teaching was classroom design. I was inspired by Kayla Dornfeld (@TopDogTeaching) years ago when she posted on her social media feeds that she was starting to roll out flexible seating. I studied more into the idea, wrote a grant, and was awarded money by the Glenview Education Foundation to try it with my students.

When the funds rolled in, I excitedly told my students about it. Together, we selected floor cushions, wobble stools, exercise balls, scoop rocker seats, and lap desks. I also found lots of great finds while shopping garage sales and visiting stores like Five Below and Michaels.

As the items arrived, we discussed safe ways to use the seating options. We collaboratively established norms and consequences. Having the students involved was important to me. Norms should never be top-down, but rather co-constructed with the team members. If I wanted students to be successful, I needed their input and investment.

As time went on, the students became experts about assessing what their needs were for each day and became aware of their bodies and overall wellness. The students were asked to reflect out loud (or sometimes on paper) about why they were electing which seating choice. The answers demonstrated high levels of reflection:

"I'm feeling good and energetic today, so I can pay attention well. I'm going to let others choose first."

"I'm feeling really tired and run-down today, so I need an exercise ball or a scoop rocker so that I can move and re-energize."

Later, the students demonstrated higher levels of empathy. Many of the students in my class that year lived in the same neighborhoods, and their apartments were very close to one another's. One morning, I watched as a conversation unfolded before me:

"Hey, I know you just picked the ball, but he needs it. He's gotta wake up a little. He was up all night. The police were in the apartment next door with the speakers going. He hardly slept."

I didn't need to intervene at all, and I watched as the kids shook hands and swapped seating choices. They knew to look out for each other and advocate for each other.

At different times throughout the year, the students were invited to make seating plan rearrangements. The students had full control—the only thing they couldn't move was our paraprofessional's desk with a desktop computer on it and our document camera table (due to their proximity to the outlet and the rules about extension cords on the floors). They'd grab a blank piece of paper and submit a design plan with a rationale. Sometimes, the rationale was simply *I'm bored with our current set-up. Let's change it.* If more than one plan was submitted at the same time, I'd pair the students together to discuss it to present to the class for their approval. The students became our interior designers.

The students were able to decide when to turn the lights on and off or to leave half of the lights on. They also had the freedom to open and close the blinds to our windows.

Why should I be the one to dictate to them what our room looked like? I wanted to ensure that their space felt like it was truly *their space.* They should be in the driver's seat, and I should be along for the ride.

STUDENT FEEDBACK

If I really want my learners to know that I'm a lifelong learner, I need them to see that I am always seeking ways to improve myself as an educator. I want them to know how much I value their thoughts, their feelings, and their input. I asked students for their feedback all the time! If we tried something new, I wanted to hear their thoughts. If we had a new book to read together, I wanted to hear what they thought of it. If I tried a new instructional strategy, I wanted to hear how it went on their end as learners!

From *The Blog: Asking Your Students for Feedback*

We know the importance of providing students with high-quality feedback. As many districts revamp their grading practices and switch to mastery-based grading systems, they are becoming increasingly aware of the value of formative assessments, using data to drive instruction, and ways to provide meaningful feedback to students.

It is equally important as we discuss ways to "empower" our students and encourage students to take ownership of their learning to allow them to provide us with feedback, too: How's it going? How's my teaching? How can I better support you?

Yes, there's a risk here. However, if we truly want to place our students in the driver's seats, we must. If we truly want to model a lifelong quest to continuously learn and prove, we must. If we want to strengthen our instruction *and* our connection to our students, we must.

ALSO— it took a lot of relationship-building over time. Keep in mind, it can be considered very disrespectful to "correct" an adult in many cultures and many homes. Students must learn and understand why you want feedback, and trust must be built before asking kids for meaningful feedback.

This can be done in a few ways, and will of course depend on your grade level, and your students' levels of language proficiencies.

I loved doing this because it showed my students that I wanted to know their thinking. I wanted to center them. I wanted my classroom to be their most exciting but also their safest. I received some harsh feedback some days, but it pushed me to be better. I didn't ask for student feedback on every lesson of course, but I did try to do this often. I never asked for student names on their papers, and I always tried to leave a space for additional comments. It normalized feedback as a part of our learning for me to ask for feedback, and they started to ask each other for feedback on their work and became more reflective thinkers in the process.

Sometimes it was just a simple thumbs-up, thumbs-down. Or sometimes they'd hold up a happy face symbol or a sad face. Other times, I'd ask them for a STAR (which meant I knew exactly what to do on this task) or a STAIR (which meant I didn't understand exactly what I needed to do—I had to keep climbing for an answer—I either had to ask a friend or ask you for more information).

I tried to match the feedback collection tool to whatever my personal instructional goal was for the week (make directions simpler and clearer, build excitement about a topic, etc.), but sometimes I just wanted to know what they were thinking on a random, rainy Tuesday.

MENTOR PROGRAM

We spend millions of dollars every year on interventions for academics. Y'all already know how I feel about academic "interventions" for multilingual learners. What do we have in place for "intervening" when our students don't feel connected?

We must have structures in place that allow all of us to prioritize the relationships we have with our students, especially those who are most vulnerable. I've read about several ways to do this, such as the A-Z list that many folks have written about: this is when the staff displays all the students' names and staff walk around with pencils or pens and write down one thing that they know about the student that's not related to academics. When they find there is a student with nothing written next to their name, the staff realizes they need to get to know that student a bit better.

In one of the middle schools I support, we designed a mentor program that allowed students to be paired with a caring adult. Teams of teachers would identify a student who may need the support of an adult at school in some capacity. Teachers and students would then meet in some way before/after school and spend time together. They would play basketball together on the playground, watch an episode of a funny show with a snack, play cards, read a book, knit, decorate and plan in a planner, build a robot, volunteer, play a board game—and so much more.

TAKING THE INSTRUCTIONAL POSTERS DOWN

There comes a dreaded time of year in every classroom in the country: state testing. We strip our students of the normalcy of our rich discussions, our lives as scientists, our journeys of reading, and make them sit in mini make-shift cubicles so they can take hours-long assessments that are biased, skewed, and meaningless.

The walls are forced to be stripped naked, removing the life and color and representations of their beautiful minds and their hard work. What's left is emptiness. It's unnatural.

Every year, I dread this. I hate stripping the walls. I hate having kids sit in bare rooms. One year, I decided to do something about it.

I reached out to all the friends we had made over the school year: local professionals, professional wrestlers, our police and fire departments, our Village president, a congressman, former teachers, future teachers, parents, university presidents, college students, and more—and I asked them for help.

I asked them for a simple selfie or a photo with a typed message that would inspire my students and encourage them. The response was overwhelming. In just a few days, I had well over 30 photos to mount to colorful construction paper and hang from the ceiling tiles on colorful rings. I waited for the first day of testing, then I put them all up after school and before school so that the kids could walk in with a little boost in confidence.

They excitedly came in with dropped jaws, threw their stuff on the floor, and proceeded to run around checking out all their well wishes from their biggest fans. All of these adults believed in them. All of these adults were in their corner. All of these adults were cheering them on. Some were folks they met in person, some were folks we knew from snail mail, and some were friends we made online.

I told them it was important that they knew that even if questions are hard today or in three years, none of our friends cared much about that. None of our friends cared about their scores. Just like in everything we do on our "normal" days, we should work hard, try our best, and enjoy learning.

MOVING BEYOND VIA REFLECTION & ACTION

Share out your reflections & action steps on Twitter using #MovingBeyondEdu

REFLECT:

- How do you want students to feel when they're in your class?

- How do you help establish a culture of lifelong learning in your classroom or school? How do you model that you are a lifelong learner?

ACT:

- How do you ask students for feedback about your classroom? How often do you do this?

Three ways to ask students for feedback:	Three times this month I can ask students for feedback:	Date I will follow up with myself: Did I ask for feedback? Did I need to make changes/adjustments based on student feedback?

Create your own inspiration wall, either digitally or physically (in your classroom or in your home). What words inspire you as an educator? Whose photos would you include? Take a photo of your Inspiration Wall and share online using #MovingBeyond!

7

BEYOND BEING CLASSMATES

BUILDING A JOYFUL CLASSROOM COMMUNITY

From The Blog: How A Lab Coat Transformed my Class

Have you ever done that activity where you ask students to draw a scientist? You don't give them any other directions, you don't load them up with background knowledge—you simply ask them to picture a scientist in their mind and draw what they see. I've also let students label the parts of a scientist (usually they'll label things like glasses, a lab coat, etc.).

I've done this for years with my third graders. Almost 90% of the time, they draw a picture of someone resembling Albert Einstein: a Caucasian old man. It took my breath away each time, and not in a good way. It troubled my heart every time the same image would surface. It also reminded me that my colleagues and I have a lot of work to do.

In October 2018, I had the pleasure of hearing from the CEO of COSI at the Ohio TESOL Conference. Frederic Bertley spoke about this troubling fact. Even more troubling was the *adults* who still envision an old white male when imagining a scientist. He then posted picture after picture and asked people in the crowd to name the scientist. Unfortunately, none of us recognized any of the pictures. He then proceeded to share with us their names, their stories, and their contributions. For example, Steve Jobs, inventor of Apple, was the son of a Syrian refugee. Google was invented by a Soviet-born American man named Sergey Brin. Do you like YouTube? Two of their three founders were immigrants: Steve Chen and Jawed Karim. Tiera Guinn is only 21 years old and during her time attending school at MIT, she worked with NASA, helping to build a space rocket. Jennifer Doudna is a professor at UC Berkeley and she developed CRISPR, which is a genetic-engineering method that may help to eradicate diseases and illnesses! Finally, Sara Seager, a female scientist born in 1971, has discovered 715 planets. What stuck with me was the fact that these were folks from diverse backgrounds: women, men, young folks, older folks, immigrants to the US, folks from around the globe, career changers, you name it! None of these folks resembled the old white man that we tend to imagine in our heads.

Every time my students shared with me their perceptions of who scientists were, it struck me that they didn't see themselves in science. It hurt. Year after year, I'd try to post pictures of scientists who look like them. We read books about diversity in science. Later, we'd try to connect with scientists in our community by writing letters or e-mailing them. We'd search how science is visible in our daily lives. We did a lot. By the next time I asked them the question (Can you draw a scientist?), they would draw all kinds of different things... which was fantastic, but it still wasn't *them*. I wanted them to see themselves.

One day I asked for friends of mine on Facebook to help me purchase lab coats for my students. I purchased two. Another four rolled in from a woman I volunteered with who was working in a STEM career. Then finally, a family member, Mary Spina, purchased an ENTIRE CLASS SET. She saw what I was trying to do, and supported my mission.

I filmed my students' reactions when I busted out the pile of beautiful new lab coats, each individually wrapped in plastic. Their eyes bugged out, they smiled, they shouted, they jumped up and down. It was such a fun and exciting day! But we didn't realize how it was going to change us and push our thinking.

Each day, we'd set the scene. Before starting science, I would tell all my students that I'd see them later on. The kids knew what this meant. They'd say goodbye to me, and then go to our storage ottoman and grab their lab coat. Some would also grab goggles if they felt inclined. They would put on their lab coats, and re-enter the classroom: this time, as scientists. They would address each other by their "doctor names" and they'd swap stories about the funny things that happened in their research last week. My little 8- and 9-year-olds turned into adults. I would sometimes take a moment and just sit back and watch them engage in their "academic scholarly talk" and be truly amazed at how my babies completely transformed. Was there an element of play? Absolutely. Was it fun? You bet.

Did it help my kids learn science?

No.

It TRANSFORMED the way my kids learned science.

I would also put on my lab coat and my "colleagues" would address me as "Doctora Spina." I chose to have a background in marine biology, so I could study manatees. Some of my short colleagues chose a background in IT, drone development, biology, cardiology, and one chose to pursue a doctorate in education (proud teacher moment!). We were all doctors of something.

Each day we would get so into it. There was a time or two where we'd be in the middle of an experience and a guest teacher would walk in to deliver a note. The first few times, we all kind of looked at each other, slightly embarrassed at the way we were carrying on. After the first initial giggles, we got used to it. We owned our scientist identities. After watching a video one day and seeing a female scientist using a clipboard, we decided we should be using those, too. So we added those to our "looks." We talked about the science behind drones, plants, cash registers, steamers at the laundromat, makeup products, cleaning chemicals, iPads, Lamborghinis, and social media. We realized that our parents (both theirs and mine) used science an awful lot in their jobs (many of which were what folks would call "blue-collar" jobs).

When science class was over, we'd say our goodbyes to our colleagues. I'll never forget one day, one young doctor remarked how busy she'd be that evening: after leaving the lab tonight, she'd have to pick up her kids and start dinner (she lamented while rolling her eyes)—this scientist was a working mom—and more power to her!

After all the lab coats were put away, we'd turn back into students and carry on with our day.

My kids learned to love science and look forward to it each day. I never felt super comfortable with teaching science before this, but I also learned to love it and look forward to these moments where we said goodbye to our student-selves and turned into scientists.

You can bet that each time we did that drawing after donning lab coats, every child did draw themselves.

Mission accomplished.

CLASSROOM INSTAGRAM

J was enamored with the teacher Instagram and Twitter worlds, and after reading *Learn Like a Pirate*, I was fully committed to having the kids monitor our classroom accounts that we'd been using to post learning for our families and connect with folks around the world. We decided to create a classroom job that would rotate each week to be our content managers. They decided when to post and what to post, or to not post at all. Some would post math lessons with our learning target, others would take a picture of a book they were enjoying. Still, others would take a picture of their favorite spot in the classroom, or a cool rock they found at recess. They'd decide on what words would accompany their post/picture. We learned about hashtags and how to search for more posts related to certain topics by using a hashtag. We learned how to tag other accounts in our posts, for example, colleges who sent us packages, etc.

As Cinco de Mayo was approaching, I read an article from *Teaching Tolerance* written by Lauryn Mascareñaz called "What is Cinco de Mayo?" (2017). I shared the article with my students, most of whom were Mexican-American. We had an honest discussion about appropriation and appreciation. We talked about misconceptions about the upcoming holiday. We asked questions to our families, friends, and students from other classes about what they knew of Cinco de Mayo. We decided to *carefully* (meaning I previewed the hashtag before the lesson and blocked certain accounts) search the hashtag #CincoDeMayo on Instagram and Twitter, and we tried to decide if the post was an example of appreciation, acculturation, or if we needed more information.

The students were able to see quite quickly as eight- and nine-year-olds how folks across the US were taking the holiday and turning it into something weird. We were all confused why someone would put a mustache decal on a baby in honor of Cinco de Mayo. It made no sense, and it was quite obvious how folks were appropriating the day.

We decided to create a chart to capture our learning and we

posted it on our social media accounts to provide some education to the world.

DIALOGUE JOURNALS

I've seen lots of educators utilize a Dialogue Journal with their students. This is a simple communication tool (either a physical or digital notebook) that is used to write messages or letters back and forth from one teacher to one student. I've seen educators use these for a variety of purposes:

1. To better connect to the student
2. To check-in with social/emotional needs by providing an outlet with a lowered affective filter
3. To continue writing development in a meaningful and engaging way

I've loved Dialogue Journaling with my students, and when I taught EL through in-class support, I found that a Dialogue Journal helped me accomplish all three of those, especially for content areas that didn't necessarily address writing (e.g.: at the time, there wasn't a lot of writing done in math in my school setting).

TEACHER BUDDIES

As my students were very talented multilingual learners and were developing in two languages simultaneously, I wanted to give them another authentic writing experience to continue developing their English writing. I asked my school staff if anyone would be interested in being a "pen pal" with a student from my class. This took a Dialogue Journal type of opportunity and gave each student their own adult to write with on a regular basis. I put a listing of my class in the staff lounge along with a brief description of their interests. By the end of the first day, my amazing colleagues filled the list, and everyone had a partner. To make things more manageable, I asked the staff to commit to sending a letter each month; however, most ended up doing more frequent notes.

What I enjoyed about Teacher Buddies' opportunity was it helped the student get to know another adult in the building. Each student had a special adult at school in their corner. Very often, the students would get a surprise note in their student mailbox at random times during the week/month from their Teacher Buddy that would lift their spirits. The students had no limitations for what they wrote, but I always offered an idea bank of things they could share. Many decided to talk about their families, their interests, what they were learning about. Others decided to share poetry or artwork with their Teacher Buddy. Sometimes, a student would invite them to Physical Education or Reading class on Tuesday the following week (sometimes without me knowing, ha!). I love that the students had someone they felt was their buddy. If our class was walking down the hall on the way to Music Class and their Teacher Buddy walked by, they would beam with pride and often give a hug or high-five as they announced to the rest of us, "That's *my* Teacher Buddy."

SELFIE SHARE

As teachers, we need to talk about moments that we are proud of and why. We need to model that we're proud of ourselves for persevering through problems and not just celebrate achievements. Students were always encouraged to take a selfie with a piece of work they were proud of and send it to whoever they wanted. Most of the time, students asked me to text a parent or guardian the picture. Other times, it was their Teacher Buddy, a celebrity on Twitter, another teacher in the building, or a previous teacher from another school. Students must learn how to celebrate their learning along the way—it's the process, not the product.

A great way to build this is to have students reflect on their work before you provide any feedback to the students. What parts were you most proud of? What part of this project pushed you? Did you ever feel like giving up? What did you do to keep going? Celebrate the moments of perseverance, not the final grades.

As more and more schools switch to standards-based grading, educators are having great conversations about feedback instead of grades. What do you find empowers your students the most?

SPINA SPA DAY

Our multilingual students have families that work hard. What I tended to hear a lot from my class was that parents were always busy and stressed.

Our society tends to glorify "the hustle." Glorifying the hustle seems to speak more towards praising privileged folks who try to continuously "level up" in life, instead of acknowledging the back-breaking labor of others that rarely results in a reward, promotion, or any other perk besides a paycheck. But, I digress.

Regardless, our students may not know when to take a break, especially if parents are not afforded that luxury. However, *this is not about us educators teaching kids what their parents can't or don't*. This is about encouraging kids to become mindful of when they need a break.

Children are just that—children. They need to be taught regulation and mindfulness. They need to become aware of their needs and their breaking points. They also must be taught skills to cope, advocate for themselves, and express their needs in a healthy way.

This is going to sound cliched because self-care is NOT about visiting the spa… it's about so much more (that we'll explore together later on!). However, after a few days of prolonged standardized testing, I could sense my kids were wearing thin and needed a break. Those winters in Chicago are not easy seasons to get through, and we can't always get outside for recess every day during the winter (especially when that windchill drops), so I knew I needed to incorporate a break of some sort that didn't involve me putting on a movie.

I printed a tiny, fancy invitation and put it in all the students' mailboxes before going home one day. I encouraged them to wear comfy clothes, but that's all I told them. The next day after testing, the students left our classroom for Physical Education, which meant that I had 25 minutes to turn our classroom into a spa.

Furniture was moved in minutes, lights went off, blankets, towels, mats, and pillows were scattered all around the room. I pulled out the Tupperware I packed earlier that day. Soft music played and a sign was placed on the door with fancy letters: Welcome to the Spina Spa. As the students returned from PE, they were invited to take off their shoes (oh yes, I'm a risk-taker asking kids to remove shoes after sweating in PE) and find a place to rest their bodies. They could choose to lie or sit in their space, whatever felt most comfortable to them. They were asked to be mindful of the volume of their voices. I whispered directions to them and invited them to help themselves to two sliced cucumbers for their eyes. My girls giggled because they said it was just like the spas on TV! The boys said NO WAY at first—that is, until one young man wanted to try it, which opened the door to all of our boys ready to try these cucumbers. After a few moments of everyone settling in and sharing the sensation of the cold cucumbers on their faces, we were ready to start a meditation.

I told my spa clients that I was going to play a meditation for kids on the speaker. They could either listen to it or just close their eyes and let their minds wander. The next 25 minutes were theirs to just relax. They couldn't play on a device, disappear into a book, or start on any homework. They just needed to rest their bodies and their minds.

After our first spa experience, the kids were hooked. We had a few more "Spa Days" throughout the year, especially during those dreaded weeks of standardized testing. Sometimes the *Spa Days* only lasted 5-7 minutes. It was awesome when kids would tell me about how they'd do this at home after a busy day at school, or how they'd ask their parents to do a meditation with them. One boy said he even treated his mom to sliced cucumbers after she got home from work one day so she could rest and feel nice. Our kids are so thoughtful!

Kids need to be explicitly taught to take breaks, rest their bodies and brains. They need to see models of this in action.

TAKING BREAKS

Our students work so hard and if they're doing *all* the content learning in addition to *all* the language learning, they may be fatigued by the afternoon. It is not uncommon for kids to say that their heads hurt by the end of the day, especially for students who are in their first few months of school in English. It's exhausting when you are constantly processing, analyzing, and searching for additional cues to aid in comprehension in another language.

We need to let kids know that it is healthy and responsible to request a break. It teaches students to become mindful of their needs, and when we honor their requests for breaks, it teaches our students that we trust them. It gives us a chance to be better listeners. We can also use that information to plan for our instructional days. Are kids typically exhausted by 10:15am? Is that a good time for a 5-minute break for everyone? Do I need to move around my schedule?

I also tried to vary up our breaks. Sometimes we did whole-group breaks where we'd all stretch, dance, or just get up and talk to each other for a few minutes. Sometimes, we'd take a walk around the building, or watch a funny YouTube video.

For individual breaks, we set up several norms towards the beginning of the year (around October). We talked about how hard we work at school and how that's something to be proud of, but we also talked about how we needed to take care of ourselves. We sometimes need to pause and ask ourselves if we are overwhelmed, or if we just need a break before moving on to the next task, or if we need to walk away from a math problem and come back to it after getting a drink of water. We talked about ways they could ask for help or ask for a break. We talked about the power in persevering through problems *and also* the benefits of coming back to something with "fresh eyes." I'd keep different things on hand, but a student favorite was bubble wrap. I kept an ongoing stash of used (but clean) bubble wrap and I'd cut it into small squares. If kids wanted a "Bubble Break," they could go grab a small square, sit somewhere in the classroom or go into the hallway and pop the bubbles. Sometimes students wanted to daydream at a desk in the hallway with a timer that would go off that let them know when they needed to come back inside the room. I told students that I couldn't decide what would work best for them, only they knew what they needed. To help, I could ask some questions that could help them in making their choices, but ultimately I wanted them to be in charge.

MEANINGFUL "BELL WORK"

I hate the term *bell work*. It already sounds meaningless, doesn't it? Work to do while waiting for the morning bell to start your school day? Eww. I used to line up worksheets in my organizational bins so I had a worksheet for each morning. When I was in the middle of a problem-solving meeting for a student, my psychologist asked if the student we were discussing could swap out his morning work for a regulation exercise to help get him ready for the day. I agreed immediately.

As I was driving home with my own kids after school that day, I thought about it some more. Do all of my students need to launch their day of learning with a worksheet? Is that what's best for eight and nine-year-olds? Would that be the most inspiring way to start the school day?

When I roll into work as an adult, I have time to put my things away, chat with my colleagues, send an email or two, fill my water bottle, and gather what I need to be successful. If my evaluator decided to give me a worksheet every morning before I was allowed to do any of those things, I would be aggravated, especially if it wasn't related to anything I was working on professionally.

After some reflection and brainstorming, I did change up our morning routine. Students had the choice of Gratitude Journaling, Reflection Writing, Work Catch Up, Dialogue Journals, or another task of their choice where they were engaging with either reading, writing, listening, and/or speaking—which has allowances for just about anything!

GRATITUDE JOURNALS

My students and I loved all things "mini." My daughter is currently in 3rd grade, and she loves the cheaper version of American Girl Doll accessories because everything is cute and small! I found that there was some novelty about using mini-notebooks for activities instead of full-sized notebooks. After seeing a picture of someone's photo on Instagram, I was inspired to try an idea myself: the teacher took a composition notebook and chopped it in half by bringing it to a home improvement store. She thought it was a great way to make her supply budget stretch, especially for her younger students who weren't composing long pieces of writing just yet. The tool of course must match the purpose, so I wouldn't use this as our Writing Notebook or our Dialogue Journal, but I thought this would be perfect as an option for a Gratitude Journal!

One of our morning routine options was to write in our Gratitude Journals. The students could fill it with bulleted lists, sentences, pictures, or paragraphs. To launch, we discussed examples of each type of gratitude expression, and I modeled it several times. We read a few statistics about how gratitude brings you more happiness and joy in your day—and who couldn't use more of that?

We talked about how gratitude wasn't necessarily about being thankful for *stuff*. Many days, we shared our gratitude lists. If we shared, it was always optional. Some frequent words included: laughter, friends, sunshine, our moms, our families, and each other.

A CONSTANT MESSAGE

We spent a lot of instructional time co-constructing anchor charts, pieces of writing, designing inspiration walls, and more. The walls of our classroom were always full, and changed when needed, but there were a few pieces that stayed up year-round, with one of my non-negotiables in particular: it must stay up all year.

It wasn't super noticeable, except towards the beginning of each school year where things tended to look a little more "blank." It was three small words that were displayed above our whiteboard, where students would look during teacher-led instruction. This sign was not co-constructed. It was a message from me to the children I served; something I always wanted them to know and remember. Three small words that I hope will always stick with them.

I am loved.

MOVING BEYOND VIA REFLECTION & ACTION

Share out your reflections & action steps on Twitter using #MovingBeyondEdu

REFLECT:

- How do you help students connect with other adults outside of the classroom?
- How do you support students in staying connected to you, each other, and others?

ACT:

- How do you help students take breaks?

I know students need a break when...	Here are three different types of breaks students can take:	How do I model the benefits of taking a break? What words or phrases might I use to students before or after a break?
1.	1.	1.
2.	2.	2.
3.	3.	3.

- How do you model celebrating yourself when you accomplish a goal? What words or phrases do you use to model your own efforts of persevering through problems or problem-solving?

I'm really excited because I recently...	I realize I need to try this again...
I'm so proud of myself for...	I'm super bummed, but now I know I need to...
I felt good about myself for...	Perhaps I need to pause and come back to this in a bit...
This weekend I was proud of...	I am going to set a timer for 15 minutes and try this one more time...

8

BEYOND OUR STUDENTS

FAMILY ENGAGEMENT

"PARENT-ONLY" EVENTS

*S*chools are sometimes strange places.

We proclaim, "We love your children," but then during certain events, we tell them that children are not allowed at this event. How child-centered are we? It's time for us to rethink the Parent-Only Events.

We send mixed messages and create barriers when we don't allow kids into events. When we don't provide options for families, it can unintentionally put a strain on families and guardians.

My sister, Danielle, has four beautiful children, and her husband often travels for work. When her family moved to Colorado, they were just getting settled into their community and were starting to get to know people. None of their family lived nearby and they didn't quite feel comfortable leaving their kids with anyone quite yet; however, the kids' schools invited parents and guardians for a Curriculum Night.

Most of us host similar events at the beginning of our school years. It gives us teachers the chance to meet all parents/guardians in person, explain the expectations of the grade level, and provide tips & tricks for navigating the school as a parent of a student in a specific grade. Typically, a lot of helpful and valuable information is shared, so most of us do what we can to encourage parents' and guardians' attendance.

When my sister got the flyer in her children's folders, on each flyer in bold letters were the words:

Children Are Not Allowed At This Event
Please Do Not Bring Your Children.

Well.

Many of us are privileged to have a friend, family member, or trusted neighbor or babysitter that we can rely on for childcare when needed, but not all of us do. My sister, who is a very loving and caring mother, had no choice but to not attend the event. This left her feeling disconnected, unwelcomed, and at a disadvantage! She worried about how best to support her kids in their respective grades in their new school community.

Are they going to stamp her kids' foreheads with "PARENTS ARE NOT INVOLVED?" Or, will the school make allowances for them because of their ability to speak English and the neighborhood they live in?

DEFINING PARENTAL INVOLVEMENT

We place a lot of judgment on the families we serve, and a lot of times it comes out of a loaded term that has many different definitions: "involved." Let's unpack this term.

To you, what does being an "involved parent" mean? To many,

it includes parents and guardians who respond to the teacher's emails, who sign up to volunteer in the classroom or school, who sign the assignment notebook each night, and who attend school events. To others, it means arriving on time for the parent-teacher conference.

We must be very clear about what this definition means because some of us could very easily declare that a particular family is "not involved." Statements like this could be a detriment to the student's learning for as long as the student attends that school. If the 4th-grade teacher shares this with the 5th-grade teacher, then the 5th-grade teacher may already have a preconceived notion of what the family is or isn't. Everyone hopes that teachers can formulate their own opinions of students in the "fresh start" of a new school year; however, it is worth noting that many of us have judgments that we tend to pass down to the next teacher that inherits our students.

When I present this topic at conferences, I always ask folks to define "parent involvement." I use a low-stakes participation tool like AnswerGarden (https://answergarden.ch/). The prompt is on the screen and participants from their seats can use the code on the screen to contribute their thoughts. The prompt is simply to define an involved parent. Over the years, some of the most frequent responses include:

- attendance at parent-teacher conferences
- showing up to school events
- volunteering in classrooms

What do you use to define parent involvement in your setting? How does your administration define parent involvement? How do your families define it? It's important to define what we're asking for so that we're all on the same page.

PARENTAL INVOLVEMENT VS. FAMILY ENGAGEMENT

There is a big difference between being "involved" and being "engaged." Most folks lean towards saying that involvement is how the parents follow the school's norms in attending events or filling out surveys. Engagement is how the school and the parents partner *with each other*. Parent involvement is great, but family engagement is much more desirable because it demonstrates that both entities have gifts, assets, talents, and value to share. It doesn't position the school and the school staff as being the all-knowing entity.

The terms *parent* and *family* are also worth noting. The term "parents" come in many forms (two moms, a single father, a legal guardian, etc.). Many children are being raised by someone other than a mother or a father; some are being raised by a grandmother or other family member. Some children are placed under the care of an appointed guardian who is not a family member. The term *family* is more inclusive. It represents whoever is raising you or playing a part in raising you, even those in temporary care. Plus, I like that the family encompasses everyone at home, including siblings and relatives who reside in the home. We can embrace and engage everyone.

CULTURAL ICEBERGS

We may all be surprised when we stop actively judging or misunderstanding each other and start learning about and with each other. We have to understand our families' cultural backgrounds and their experiences and expectations of the role of the school and the role of the family.

Did you know that some parents won't ask you questions at the parent-teacher conference because they feel that it would come across as disrespectful? To them, it may seem off-putting and show that they don't trust you or they're questioning you or your actions as the teacher. To you, you may be feeling that they're aloof or uninvolved for not asking questions. Do a quick google search of cultural iceberg graphics and discuss them in teams prior to parent-teacher conferences or family events.

"BROKEN FAMILIES"

Enough with this phrase. You don't get to decide which families are broken and which ones are not. Please choose a different phrase when you're talking with colleagues about anyone's families.

Isn't it funny how so many will use the African proverb, "It takes a village to raise a child," but then judge that village up and down because it doesn't resemble theirs? Sometimes the village is a single mom, or a single dad, or an aunt and uncle, or grandparents. Let's respect the village and support it instead of declaring it broken.

OBSTACLES

Have you considered the reasons why families did not attend the school function or the parent-teacher conference? As in, have you asked them? You don't want to send a letter home asking why they didn't come to the school picnic, but you could always have a conversation with any willing family who'd be willing to offer feedback either to you or to the school.

Once my teammates and I became more aware of our families' needs, we learned a lot about many of the common obstacles that could potentially stand between us coming together.

1. Childcare
2. Transportation
3. Access to language support
4. Confidence, Clear Purpose, & Clear Expectations

Digging deeper, we realized that there were some big steps that our schools needed to do to allow parent involvement to happen.

We need to address those "Parent-Only" school events. First of all, let's ask ourselves why kids can't be in the same room when parents are learning about the classroom at the beginning of the year? Are we divulging secret information that isn't acceptable for children's ears? Probably not. This could be a great opportunity to talk about school schedules, share tips & tricks, discuss what to expect in class this year, share a calendar of events in advance, and allow for students and their parents alike to ask questions.

If childcare is an obstacle for families you serve, ask your school about opening up different sections of the school to host childcare. Ask staff members who aren't presenting information to run the rooms. Break them apart by grade level or grade level clusters, and plan a special and engaging activity for students. Be sure to put that information on your promotions, flyers, and social media posts about the event: *Free Childcare By School Staff Available! Go Ahead & Bring the Kids if You Need To!* Read books, host a dance party, play with robots, or do some yoga. It's a great opportunity to try something different with kids and form relationships with siblings who have not yet entered our schools, or reconnect with former students who have moved up to other schools. This ensures that the childcare is safe and trusted by parents, and kids will not feel nervous with an unfamiliar adult.

If transportation is an obstacle for families you serve, see if you can employ a carpool system for families who live nearby each other. This could be a simple note at the end of an RSVP to an event:

- No, I can't attend the event, but thanks!
- I can attend and I can drive others. I live near
  _____.

- I would like to attend but I need a ride. I live near
  _____.

Another option is to enlist staff to pick up families on their way to the event. You can also see if there are funds for the school or district to provide a bus to pick up families along already-existing bus routes.

If access to language support is an obstacle for families you serve, there's still a lot you can do! Build lots of comprehensible input into the way you promote your events. Simplify the language and avoid putting too much on the flyer: date, location, start time, end time, a line for transportation, and that's it! Keep it short and simple. You can also record videos or add audio files to enhance your message so that families who may not have literacy skills yet can still access the information. Be sure to engage your language liaisons, and that your invitations/flyers/posts are translated into your school's most frequent languages. Talk to your students about the events so that they can explain it to parents if they share the same language skills. Don't stop with the invitation; also employ the same supports for the event itself. Hire interpreters, bring in volunteers, keep messaging simple, allow parents to write comments in their native language. (You can later utilize transla-tors who can translate the message or question into English for you). Ensure that during the event, multilingual folks are easily identifiable with something like a button on their lanyard or a sign above their station that says in which language they can receive help/support/directions. Seeing "Hablo español" on a button may be the entry point for a relationship, or at least an opportunity to help in a small moment.

If confidence is an obstacle for families you serve, there's a lot you can do to provide support. Provide families with a map of the school with a highlighted hallway. Show them in a video where to park and what time to arrive; give them that insider tip of where to park if the lot is full. A few days in advance, make a video of yourself walking down the hallway, turning the corner, and finding your classroom. Offer to meet them in the parking lot and walk into the school with them. Tell them what time the event starts and what time it ends. Tell parents it's okay if they are running late —you'd still love their presence! Dress in comfortable clothing and encourage them to do the same. Tell them you're going to wear jeans and gym shoes because this isn't a formal event. Tell them how the night will be laid out (*e.g., I'll talk for 10 minutes, give you a chance to ask questions, and then we'll write a letter to the kids. After that, you can feel free to explore the classroom and school, talk with other parents, or feel free to head home!*). Tell parents that they can look for staff members with blue flags that are stationed around the school if they need help finding a classroom.

PARENTS/GUARDIANS AS VOLUNTEERS

There are a lot of ways that parents can volunteer at school, but how inclusive are our practices around volunteering? In what ways are we able to break down barriers so that interested parents/guardians can volunteer at school? How are we creating volunteer opportunities as children age into middle school and high school?

Kristy Patterson, an EL Network Specialist for the Office of Language and Culture in Chicago Public Schools, says: "Inviting multilingual parents into the schools to volunteer amplifies their leadership at home, at school, and in the community. The goal should be to make parents experts in their child's school and part of a community of leaders. This then leads to filling equity gaps by involving parents directly with the school, teachers, and administrators. Multilingual parents feel accepted and comfortable and are more inclined to continue to participate throughout their child's education."

Examine the ways in which your school asks for volunteers. Is the communication only sent in English? Is the communication only sent via email? If so, you'll only get English-speakers with Internet access who use email on a regular basis, which means that the kids, staff, and community will only see monolingual parents volunteering. This can paint a dangerous narrative.

Does the communication include multiple avenues and clearly lay out the description of the volunteer commitment? For example, being a mystery reader for an English story requires English literacy skills. Look for a mystery reader in other languages. It's a beautiful thing when students are able to hear parents reading in their heritage language. I love being read to in all languages, even those I don't understand!

LIVE STREAMING THE SPEAKER ONLINE

Check your school's policy on streaming your parent night information for those who are unable to make it in person. If the video is set on just filming YOU and not the parents attending (or any kids who may be present), it may be allowable. This can be done in private Facebook groups by doing a video (i.e., Facebook Live, or by doing a Zoom/Google Meet/Microsoft Teams) meeting with a special code. This allows more accessibility by those who cannot attend in person. *Since we're all experts at using these tools now, why would we not do this in the future?*

BPAC

In the state of Illinois, schools must create and maintain a Bilingual Parent Advisory Committee, or BPAC, when there is a bilingual program in existence. I love this and think every school needs one, whether or not it is required! The purpose is to allow parents to inform the bilingual program, make decisions, and evaluate the program. Per state law, they must meet four times per year and they must have parent representation as well as school personnel as they launch. They later switch to being a parent-led and parent-operated structure within the school system. This is a powerful way to engage our linguistically diverse families that we serve by providing a dedicated space to share their reflections and guide programs while having a leadership role in the school system. While we need our parents at this table, we need our parents at *every* table, and it's on us to create those avenues if they aren't yet there. For more information, you can review the Illinois State Board of Education website at www.isbe.net.

PARENTAL ASSOCIATIONS: WHO'S REPRESENTED?

Another channel that most schools have is the Parent-Teacher Association, or PTA (some school districts have other names for similar parent groups). This is a good group to use as a systems check. Scan the next PTA meeting and reflect: In what language(s) are your PTA meetings run? Does everyone around the table look the same? Is there equity of voice? Do all parents know that this organization exists, and is it easy for them to join? To accommodate working parents, can meetings also be streamed online in a private group with a code that is shared? See what you can do to increase linguistic diversity around the table. Ensure that the meeting information goes out in more languages, and let families know that you will have interpreters available at the next few meetings, along with which topics will be discussed. Putting dates out for the meetings well in advance will also help folks who are interested in joining.

BOARD OF EDUCATION MEETINGS

By doing some reflecting, we can identify how welcoming or how accessible information is to all families that we serve. If this is the decision-making group of individuals in our school districts, then our parents must all feel welcome, invited, and included. Here are some reflection questions that you may want to consider:

- In what language(s) are your local Board of Education meetings run?
- In what language(s) are the meeting minutes sent out?
- How are the meetings made public?
- Who is attending the meetings and who is not?
- Even more notable, check out the Board itself: Who is on it? Do they all look the same?

CLASS PROJECTS ARE PRICEY

School projects can be fun and are a great way for kids to learn longer-term time management skills and show their learning in a unique way.

But... I will admit it: as a mom, I hate projects. I do. I wish I could change that about myself, but I just hate them. Here are some of the reasons why:

1. They always require strangely specific items that I can never find, and that I don't have on hand at home. There's usually some sort of note that goes along with the directions that say something like, "Don't worry parents! Most of these things you already have on hand at home. You'll simply need 46 green pipe cleaners, 13 googly eyes, 34 small pom poms in different colors, 17 red popsicle sticks, goat's blood, and a live chipmunk." This usually means a few trips to the craft stores, where I throw a fit because the popsicle sticks are only sold in a set of 12 with only 4 red ones inside, so I have to end up buying 5 packs.
2. They're expensive. Once we had to make a dwelling for my son's 5th-grade project. It cost me about $60.
3. As a learner, I never liked art, projects, or making things with my hands. I'm telling you this because *most of us tend to teach in the way that we learned best when we were students!* Yikes! What about all my students who like to do projects?
4. It always ends up in a fight between my child and me. Seriously. It starts so nice, and as we lay out all of our newly purchased supplies on the table, I take a deep breath and I think *Wow, maybe I could be one of those*

Pinterest-moms after all. Twelve minutes later, the truth is revealed. We are fighting because the glue won't hold the pom poms onto the popsicle stick, the table is sticky, and our project looks nothing like the model that we were given.

From the Blog: Is this Project Respectful of My Families?

During my first year as a 3rd-grade classroom teacher, I learned an important lesson.

There seemed to be an expectation to assign big projects. I'm talking about BIG PROJECTS. For instance, I wrote home asking families to construct a 3D design of a Chicago landmark as a culmination to our social studies unit on the study of Chicago. I attached the rubric and had it translated into English/Spanish. I went over the rubric in great detail with my students. I gave them lists of recycled materials that they could use. I showed them great samples of models other kids constructed that I found online. We viewed photos and videos of the landmarks together. I had visions in my head of a classroom full of beautiful models representing our wonderful city...

Over the next two weeks, I held class meetings where we discussed our check-ins on the project. The students all verbally shared the status of their projects and assured me that things were going along great! Our collective excitement grew to have our big reveal!

Well, those two weeks went by quite quickly. The Big Day arrived. I greeted the kids at the exterior door to find one student in line holding a large project. One. I smiled and looked around the students, trying to see if a parent was nearby holding their project for them, or seeing if they placed it against the wall to ensure it didn't get messed up. I shrugged, figuring that they had engineered something that is tucked neatly in their backpacks and requires a few simple pieces of construction once inside the classroom.

After the students unpacked, attendance was taken, and our morning mantra was recited, I asked my wonderful students to take out their projects. As I looked around the room, no one moved a muscle. They all glanced around at each other. Some reported that they forgot theirs at home.

Embarrassingly, my first instinct was to become frustrated. After TWO WEEKS to work on this, I had ONE model in my classroom. ONE! Ugh!

I looked around the room. I looked at the expressions on the faces of the students. I saw shame, embarrassment, and guilt.

Because of me. This was on me.

You see, when projects like these are assigned, there are assumptions made:

1. There is an adult at home to assist their child and also understand the large project.

2. There are supplies (scissors, crayons, tape, etc.) at home for the student to utilize to complete the project.

3. The student has "recyclable materials" on hand. I later learned that many of my students didn't have empty cereal boxes at home because they either don't eat cereal regularly or the cereal they ate came in bags. I could have easily collected cereal boxes for my students to use if I had thought to ask my students. I made assumptions about what my students had at home based on the things that I had at home.

4. The student has excellent time management skills or tools were provided to help them manage the project with a level of independence.

5. The student has developed self-advocacy skills and knows how to ask the teacher for help.

I was guilty of making all of these assumptions. But now? I know better, so I do better. Here are some ways that I can ensure that I'm being respectful of my students and their families when assigning large projects.

1. Can my students complete this in class? By giving them time during class, they will have access to supplies, materials, and support. This also lifts the burden off my families, many of whom are working multiple jobs or working nights.

2. What materials and supplies can I send home? By sending home both materials AND supplies, I can ensure that everyone has what they need to be successful. It also lifts the demand for parents to purchase items that may not be in their budget.

3. Can I call home to talk with parents about this project?

By making personal contact with my families, I can ensure that everyone understands the project. I can also find out if anyone needs any additional support, ideas to better the project, or a deadline extension. Things come up, so by opening up the lines of communication, I'm sharing the responsibility with the parent/guardian of the student.

4. Did I provide a timeline or checklist? By providing this often overlooked tool, I am providing support to students who need manageable chunks to complete larger-scale projects.

5. Are there multiple ways for my students to express their learning? Why must they do the project in this way? By allowing multiple ways for students to express their learning, it allows them to be creative. We as teachers mustn't get caught up in the "my whole team is doing it this way" hype. Always consider your WHY.

6. Ask yourself, "Is this project placing a burden on my families in any way?" For example... Are they expected to visit a library to complete this project or a craft store? Do they have reliable transportation during library or craft store hours? Do they have the time to do this? Will they have to drag all their young siblings along to get this done?

By being respectful of our families, we can ensure that our students will be and feel successful and remove those moments of shame and guilt!

PACKETS

I haven't ever met a packet that I enjoyed completing. Packets are not very motivating or inspiring. The only thing that packets teach us is that we all hate packets. There are a lot more engaging ways to learn content rather than filling out endless amounts of worksheet after worksheet. Kids don't feel empowered by packets. Parents don't feel all that enthused, either.

OTHER UNNECESSARY BURDENS

What else can we eliminate or at least do some more reflecting about?

I used to make my students fill out their assignment notebooks each day. There was a space at the bottom for the parent to sign the assignment notebook. Folks assured me that this was THE WAY to ensure that parents knew about which assignments were due. This was THE WAY to ensure that parents could help their students stay organized. In the mornings, I told kids to come on in and open their assignment notebooks so I could check to see which parents signed it. Ugh. But wait, it gets worse.

Enter the reading log: are we requiring parents to sign or initial the same piece of paper every single day? Why? For added compliance or increased accountability? Guess what? Some parents (like myself) signed the paper even when my child hasn't read for 20 minutes. GASP! I know. I'm such a rebel. The truth is, I value my kids' reading lives, but sometimes we're busy running to the craft store to buy $60 worth of supplies and we just didn't have time to read for more than 12 minutes that day. Hopefully, I don't get labeled as an "uninvolved parent" or have my kids be identified as having "little support at home" on all their transition notes for next year's teacher.

Let's be reflective of the purpose of all those little things that seem like little things to us but are actually small burdens.

PARENT-TEACHER CONFERENCES

Here are a few considerations for planning parent-teacher conferences.

- Offer flexibility in time and location: While meeting face-to-face is ideal, let families know that you can accommodate their schedules. We shouldn't have to make parents take a day off of work to accommodate a parent-teacher conference. We don't know how stable their job is or how that day's lack of pay would impact the family or their budget. It's also none of our business. Offer to meet them at a local coffee shop, do a phone conference, or participate in a video conference.
- Timing: If you are asking parents/guardians to come to the school building, don't only talk to them for 10 minutes. That hardly seems worth it. I once heard about a mom who walked 1.5 miles in the August heat to meet with a teacher only to be given 10 minutes to talk about school supplies. The mom then had to turn around and walk the 1.5 miles back home. Ugh. That could have been a phone call.
- Tone: Ensure that the experience is a positive one. Don't bombard parents with test scores and benchmark data. Be mindful of what type of information you are sharing with parents. If you are sharing data, be sure that you are explaining what the data means. Not all parents are familiar with all of

our assessments and what each of the scores means. Also, don't forget to share linguistic data with parents!

- Avoid Edu-Lingo. As educators, we swim in acronyms and educational jargon. Think of it as our technical vocabulary. Let's avoid the jargon and speak from the heart instead.

- Help prepare families by letting them know in advance what types of things to expect at a parent-teacher conference. Every school does things a little differently, and if your families are from another country, it is possible that this looked vastly different or is new altogether. Let them know where to park, what time to arrive, and even what to do if there is another conference being wrapped up when they arrive. Encourage them to bring questions and schedule in time for them to ask questions, but don't be offended if they don't ask any.

STOP PLANNING EVENTS IN MAY, SERIOUSLY!

School calendars in May are explosive. There is so much packed into one month, and while it's a great time of year to celebrate a year of learning, it does call for some reflection.

My husband and I both work full-time in addition to raising our two children. Every single week in May, our school calendars are full of events. There's a book fair, a concert series, a Mother's Day event (and many schools often do a Fathers' Day event in preparation), a Field Day, a spirit week of some sort, a play, an art show, a musical, a Teacher Appreciation event, an open house, a bake sale, a school scavenger hunt, and an ice cream social event.

I'm already tired at the end of my workday, but then I have to magically accommodate every event in my kids' schedules to feel like a successful parent. It's exhausting!

Take a peek at your school's calendar and make adjustments. Which events can take place at another time during the year? Which events can be combined (or gasp!—*canceled*)? While it's great to celebrate learning at the end of a school year, let's remember that learning happens every day all year long. Let's put less focus on products and more focus on process and progress! Let's consider the *purpose* of each of those events.

MOTHER'S DAY EVENTS

Every family looks different. Some families have 2 moms, 1 mom, 0 moms, 4 mother-like figures, etc. Mother's Day may also be a difficult day for many, including the colleagues we work with each day. Mother's Day in the US is celebrated at a different time than Mother's Day in other countries. Do a quick Google search and see! We don't necessarily have to celebrate it the same way that we did as children. Why not change the event to be more inclusive—perhaps a *Celebrate a Woman Day*? Invite or celebrate a special woman of your choice. The same thing goes for Father's Day.

SPIRIT WEEK AND THE STRESSOR ON FAMILIES

Monday: Crazy Hair Day
Tuesday: Wear Cerulean Pants Day
Wednesday: Chicago Bulls Day
Thursday: Twin, Triplet, & Quadruplets Day
Friday: Wear Long Tie-Dye Socks Day

Lots to say here.

1. "Crazy Hair" can be problematic. For many kids, this may mean using hair chalk in different colors and using 14 scrunchies in their hair. For some kids, this may mean a very intricate style that the parent or guardian found on Pinterest. Sounds harmless, right? "Crazy Hair Day" can take a turn real fast when a student chooses to use a hairstyle commonly used predominantly by one racial group (such as braids, dreadlocks, cornrows) as a means of being "crazy" and disrespects an entire ethnicity. This also requires that an adult or older sibling is home and available on Monday morning before school to do something different with their child's hair. What about students who don't show their hair? What about students who have alopecia?

2. Wear Cerulean Pants Day or whatever random and hard-to-find color on whatever article of clothing is asked. I don't have additional funds to fork over to Target for something my child will only wear once, nor the time to bounce to different retailers to find a cerulean pair of pants in their size that meets their sensory needs on the night before Wear Cerulean Pants Day. Instead, maybe kids can just wear their favorite color on that day.

3. We don't own a lot of Chicago Bulls gear. I think there's a shirt or two here and there, but just because we live in a city that favors a team doesn't mean that everyone has access to a t-shirt that represents the logo of that team. Plus, have you seen how overpriced the merchandise is that boasts the official logo of sports teams? Yikes! Unless it was on my child's birthday list from three months ago, we probably don't have that item. Instead, perhaps students can pick a sport or

team of their choice to represent if they want to participate.

4. Twins, Triplets, Quadruplets, Whatever Day assumes that everyone has a BFF or a social group. What kind of social anxiety does this create for kids who don't feel connected? It also assumes that everyone has the means (like the time and money) to plan coordinating outfits in just days. If the folks in your social circle all have varying socioeconomic means, and they all pick certain brands to wear and you don't have it and can't afford it, are you out? After all, teachers aren't monitoring this. Do families now have to stay up late and do laundry or visit the laundromat to be sure that those particular items are clean and ready to be worn?

5. Wear Long Tie-Dye Socks Day: I have heard friends say that this is generally meant to be a money-saver for families who can't afford the other "days" to participate. That statement itself is problematic, to begin with, but I'll just stay focused on this spirit day for now. *This is easy for parents to do and make at home! What a fun, shared learning experience this can be for families! Yay!* Wrong. Unless you're supplying the long socks, the tie-dye kit, the time, the directions, *and* the adult supervision required, this experience is not in any way an "equalizing" experience.

Anytime a family is asked to stretch their hard-earned dollars to accommodate their child's participating in a school community-building experience such as a spirit day, we are creating a further divide between the Haves and the Have-Nots. What is the purpose of the week to begin with—to have fun while building feelings of connectedness and belonging, or is it to flaunt wealth and privilege?

While we're on the topic of Spirit Days, let's also be careful of some rather obvious missteps: don't ever ask your students to "dress like a (insert cultural group here)." Yikes. It's even problematic if we were to say "Dress like an American."

Number one: I wish there was a word in the English language to say United States-ian. When we say *American*, there is North America, Central America, and South America.... I understand that this country is called The United States of America, but it still feels weird.

Number two: If the goal is to promote patriotism or pride for the US, you can instead say that interested folks can dress in red, white, and blue. Plus, how do folks in the US dress? I was born in the US and I don't dress in red, white, and blue every day.

I promise I'm not trying to suck the fun out of your fun-filled week, but we can all be considerate of what we're asking or promoting.

FEEDBACK NIGHT, Q&A SESSIONS, & COMMUNITY FORUMS

During those seasons of time where school districts ask the parent/guardian community for feedback, they will host community forums. They may ask for public input on an upcoming initiative, program, referendum, investment, etc. Sometimes school districts will house informational evenings to discuss the possibility of beginning a full-day kindergarten program instead of continuing their half-day programming. Perhaps the district is exploring dual language programming and they'd like to inform the parent community about the benefits. I've seen lots of school districts in Illinois host opportunities for a Question & Answer session so that they can communicate a particular goal, clarify any misconceptions, and ask for public support. Whenever we are hosting forums like these, we should ask ourselves what evidence is there that feedback is being sought out from everyone, not just English speakers with Internet access, childcare, and transportation?

OUR COMMITMENT TO ALL FAMILIES

I used to say that we owe it to our linguistically diverse families to provide them the most access and opportunity possible because many worked hard to send their children to schools here. I have now reflected on that and I now find my former thinking problematic, because *all families* deserve all the access and opportunity possible. Period. They didn't need to *earn it* because of how hard they worked. *It may not have been a choice* for many to wind up here in our schools. War, poverty, abuse, or traumas may have led to families residing within our school boundaries. We cannot assume that this was someone's ultimate goal. We owe this to our families because *they are all families that we serve.*

Just as we proclaim that all students are our students, we must also proclaim just as loudly and with just as much heart that we serve all families, not just the ones that look like us and speak our language. We must call ourselves out on our biases, seek to actively form positive relationships, and look for opportunities to increase access and opportunities for us to partner with our families that we serve. Go ahead and be that teacher that raises their hand at the staff meeting to ask if the document will be translated. Go ahead and email that administrator to ask if interpreters will be available at the upcoming school concert. Go ahead and ask your teammates if the class project may be assuming a privilege at home.

Ensure that they have a seat at the table and a voice in the decision-making. Remember that we are not trying to BE their voice, we are trying to AMPLIFY their voice. We are not trying to speak *for* them, we are trying to ensure that they have the platform to speak for themselves, with our support when needed. I don't know anyone that feels that their school or district hits this mark 100% of the time, but I do know lots of change agents, educators, and leaders who are working hard on improving themselves and their systems. Let's celebrate our successes along the way, and keep on pushing and advocating for all of our families.

We cannot claim to be child-centered if we don't support our families.

MOVING BEYOND VIA REFLECTION & ACTION

Share out your reflections & action steps on Twitter using #MovingBeyondEdu

REFLECT:

- Do you feel that your parent groups are representative of all families in your school community? Why or why not? What barriers may your school system need to address?

ACT:

- How do you define family engagement? How do your teammates and administrators define it? How do the families you serve define it?

Family Engagement

I define it as....	My families define it as:	My colleagues define it as...	My administrators and leaders define it as...
It can include things like: * * * *	It can include things like: * * * *	It can include things like: * * * *	It can include things like: * * * *

- How do you ensure that families have access to school events?

☐ Transportation
☐ Childcare
☐ Translated invitation
☐ Invitation in multiple formats (text message, newsletter, email, paper flyer, audio message, video announcement etc.)
☐ Interpreters available

9

BEYOND THE NEWSLETTER

EFFECTIVE COMMUNICATION PRACTICES

*W*e talk a lot about relationships with kids, but we don't invest the same amount of time in having conversations about the relationships we have with the families we serve. After all, we can't claim to be child-centered if we don't support our families.

"THE HARD TO REACH FAMILIES"

I've been a part of many meetings where someone asks how to engage hard-to-reach families, and I'm sure you have been, too. Many times, it is expressed as frustration:

- "Families in that neighborhood don't come to events."
- "Our _____-speaking families tend to not come to the conferences."

I'm sure you could list a few other statements that you've heard (or even said) before at a meeting.

This is a good time to practice a pause. As practitioners, it is important for us to be reflective of these statements. Are these words rooted in assumptions that are made about entire groups of people based on the neighborhood they live in or the language they speak?

If we were to engage the families in a conversation about why they didn't attend the parent-teacher conference, we may have some good opportunities for growth. Many times, we didn't even invite the families to begin with. For example, if the communication home from my kid's school was a paper sent home in a folder written in Bulgarian, and I can't read in Bulgarian, I probably will ask my child a question about it or I'll throw it away, because if I don't understand it—*then it's just a piece of paper,* it's not an invitation for me to attend a parent-teacher conference.

The "Hard to Reach Families" may not be hard to reach at all. It is natural for us to continue practices that we grew up with based on our own experiences. However, it is imperative that we pause and reconsider some of the habits we've developed or inherited from our school systems. Perhaps we were going about things the wrong way. Let's take this as a moment of reflection and an opportunity to improve our practices.

COMMUNICATION

If my workplace didn't require me to check my email so often, I'd probably never use it. Truly. These days, we have so many different methods that we use to communicate, it seems weird to only use a few when communicating with the families we serve. Find out which methods they prefer. You cannot get upset with a family when they don't respond to your email if it isn't something they use every day. One of your first notes home or your first face-to-face encounter with your families can be a discussion of how they prefer to talk to you. You can set it up as a list with checkbooks, or a list where they had to highlight their top three communication preferences. Some things you may want to include:

- Text messages
- Emails
- Phone calls
- Flyers & notes in kids' folders or backpacks
- Our Closed Facebook Group for our Class
- Weekly paper newsletters
- Weekly digital newsletters (with videos/audio embedded for accessibility)
- Our classroom Twitter account (Direct Messaging available)
- Our classroom Instagram account (Direct Messaging available)
- Seesaw posts
- Other: _____

You'll also want to remind families that you will continue to share information through certain methods/platforms, but you will honor their preferences as much as you possibly can. It's important to note that the school and the principal may send out a weekly newsletter or special announcements in a few different ways, so they can continue to check those avenues as well.

If you have concerns about giving out your personal number to families, you can use Google Voice to create a different phone number that can connect to your phone. Talking Points is a great application for your phone that you can use to set up a different phone number and send messages in a multitude of languages.

They are translated instantly for you. The translations are not perfect as it is powered through technology, but attempts to communicate in the language of the family is powerful and appreciated.

I'll also go ahead and throw in a disclaimer to check in with your school's or district's communication policy.

THAT FIRST PARENT NIGHT

There are always first-day jitters when students start that first day of school. I always have butterflies myself before my students pour into class on the first day. The same is true for that first parent night. In my case, our district calls it a Curriculum Night. The purpose of the evening is for parents to come to school and meet the teacher to learn about that grade's standards, classwork, homework and behavior expectations, and loads of other topics.

It's that first night to make an impression on the parents and guardians you serve. A question I always asked myself is, **"How do I want my parents to feel when they leave?"**

If I gave the parents packet after packet of the third grade standards, it may feel overwhelming. It may not feel very meaningful. If I gave the parents a rule book, it may feel like I'm a compliance monster. If I gave the parents a 30 minute PowerPoint presentation, they may feel bored and uninspired.

I decided that I want my families to leave my classroom feeling excited that their child is in my class. I want families to know that I'm here for their child, but also there for them, too. When my families leave my classroom, I want them to feel like they know I will work hard for their students, push them hard, try new things with them, and have fun.

This reflection shaped my "presentation" that I delivered. I played lively music, had some snacks out, and set out a blanket with soft toys and Duplo Legos at the front and the back of the classroom, in case anyone needed to bring in their baby or toddler and wanted to sit on the floor with them. I set out some coloring books and crayons in case anyone needed to entertain their kids.

You'll need to note that the school was very strict in communications about not bringing kids to this "parent-only" evening (yes, yes—big eye roll here), but I told parents and the kids that all are welcome in room 9 and no one will be asking them to leave.

We talked about some of the cool things I wanted to do and try with the students that year. We talked about special events that the school does and I asked if they had ideas for things they wanted to try. I gave parents time to download Instagram and Twitter if they hadn't had it previously and did a brief tutorial for how to use them (although most parents were already using Instagram). I also had parents take out their cell phones and enter in my contact information during the presentation. I also spent some time talking about communication preferences, and I'd give them a list of reasons why they may want to reach out to me.

I didn't do this for my entire teaching career, but in my most recent years, this is a practice I have found so valuable, especially as an educator serving linguistically diverse families. Every culture and each family of every culture has expectations of what the teacher or school is supposed to. Every culture and each family of every culture has expectations of what the parent's role in education is supposed to be.

From the Blog: Why Contact the Teacher?

Because each family may have a different understanding of why they can reach out to their child's teacher, I like to supply families I serve with reasons why they can reach out to me. This helps me to be a better connector to resources and a better support to families. Here is a sample letter I typically send to families at the beginning of the year. Sometimes I'll resend it throughout the year as a great reminder of ways I can support them.

Hi Families!

I'm so glad I get to be your child's teacher this year. Don't forget—we are partners all year long! You can call me, email me, or text me anytime. Here are a few reasons why you may want to reach out, but remember, there are many ways that we can partner, and I want to learn from you and hear your ideas, too.

When to call Mrs. Spina...
*When I want to share a great story about my child or my family
*When my child does something great and I need to tell someone about it
*When I want to teach Mrs. Spina, the class, or the school a special skill
*When I want to help in the classroom or the school
*When I have a great idea I want to share
*When I want to share how my family celebrates birthdays, a holiday, or an event
*When I have a question about school, the neighborhood, or our town
*If I want to brainstorm ways to motivate my child
*If I want to brainstorm ways to celebrate my child

*If I need help finding resources/books to keep my child reading in our home language
*If my child is struggling with school work
*If my child is struggling with behavior
*If my child is interested in a new sport/activity, but I don't know how to sign them up
*If I need help finding the library or getting a library card
*If I need some help or have questions about the food pantry
*If I want to join the PTA
*If I want to attend a Board of Education meeting
*If I want to schedule a meeting with the principal, social worker, or another teacher and I need help
*If my child seems more sad than usual
*If I have a concern about school
*If I need more support for my family
*If I need help or support for myself

Even if I don't have the answer right away, I will help you or connect you to the right person or resource. I'm dedicated to being a supportive resource to your entire family!

Sincerely,

Mrs. Spina

I'd have that letter printed 2-sided in English and Spanish so that parents could choose whichever language they felt most comfortable reading. Keep in mind, I did this when teaching in a bilingual English/Spanish classroom.

During that first night together, I'd always reiterate that I'm a mom also and I often have questions about my own kids and their learning, so I talk to my kids' teachers a lot. I'd give parents information about the Parent and Teacher Association (PTA), our Bilingual Parent Advisory Council, and our days off of school. I would tell them that their individual and collective voice mattered at our school.

I'd finish the night telling the parents that I'm so excited to be their kids' teacher this year. I tell them that I just really want their kids to be happy when they're at school. To end the night, we'd take a giant group selfie that I'd show the kids tomorrow at school, and I'd invite all the parents to write their child a note. For whichever parents were unable to attend, I'd stay for a few minutes later, after all the parents had left, and write a quick note to the child from me.

I always felt successful if my parents would smile or laugh. I felt extra successful if other parents popped their heads in to join us in our fun with our music and snacks, or if a colleague would comment about all the laughter they heard. (Did I mention I am a *very loud* laugher? I'm the loudest, *seriously*.)

SOCIAL MEDIA AS A MEANS TO CONNECT

As I mentioned earlier in this book, I loved utilizing social media with the students I served because it provided so many benefits and opportunities. One of these was the ability to connect with families in powerful ways without adding an email to their inboxes or a paper in their folders. Our learning was documented and shared often and almost always was accompanied by a picture or video.

This has allowed parents to provide access to students' learning in profound ways.

For any family, whether they are multilingual or not, to see what's inside their child's classroom can be an inside look at what learning looks like in schools today in our system. I have conversations all the time with my mom and dad about how different schools are today from when they were in elementary school. Parents all have had such varied experiences of school, no matter where they're from. Just ask any parent about Common Core Math and you'll see what I mean!

Even if families have varying levels of literacy skills, a picture is worth a thousand words. If social media is a platform that they're already utilizing to stay connected with their friends and families, it makes sense for us to connect with them on an already-familiar platform instead of getting frustrated when they don't learn about the platforms the school paid for and uses. Social media is something that many folks check when they're on work breaks or waiting for an appointment.

One of the most notable things here is that while Internet services are expensive, and many of the families I served didn't have access to laptops or WiFi, they did have data plans on their cell phones. This is why email wasn't a preferable mode of communication for many—they preferred texting or social media.

There are all kinds of things that you can do in your settings to keep your accounts private. Again, please check with your district's policies before utilizing these platforms, and never post a student's name alongside their photo.

One of the coolest moments for me was when a student's uncle who lived in Mexico City was able to write a note of congratulations on his nephew's math test picture on our classroom Instagram account. I'll never forget how much it brightened his day to hear from his beloved uncle that he hadn't seen in a few years.

POSITIVE INTERACTIONS

I can tell when someone is looking down on me. They talk over me. They don't even look at me when they speak and instead look at everyone else. When I make a statement it's quickly brushed off or my point is negated somehow. They don't smile at me and they don't treat me with warmth. Sometimes they are downright condescending.

If you told me that there was an event where that person would be and I was invited to come with you as a guest, I'd probably decline or make up a reason I can't go. If that person was inviting me themselves, I'd decline the invitation. No thanks!

How many of our families have had experiences talking to teachers or administrators who look down on them?

Relationships are built on small, positive interactions that continue over time. Let's explore some of the small, positive interactions that we can build with our families.

Positive calls home are a beautiful way for us to express how much we care for each family's child. Sharing something positive, no matter what it is, shows families (and the student) that we are proud of them! We see the work they are doing, we see how kind they are, we see how special they are! What parent or guardian doesn't want to receive some good news about their child?

> BONUS: Engage your Language Liaison Bank of folks who can make phone calls on your behalf if you don't speak an additional language besides English. We'll explore this more in our next chapter, but in the meantime, find out which staff in your school speak an additional language and feel comfortable making phone calls home. Make it

easy on your school staff and have them fill out a simple Google Form that asks for the student's first and last name, the compliment, and the language the family prefers to communicate in—then connect that form to the language liaison! Any adult can submit a compliment. Tally your numbers and share them out with your school to encourage more participation: *Hey Team—this week our school made 16 positive phone calls home in English, 18 in Tagalog, 3 in Romanian, and 21 in Spanish! Keep spreading joy next week!* I'd also encourage your language liaisons to share the parents' reaction with whichever adult submitted the compliment: *Mrs. Bishop was so excited to hear that her daughter participated in music class this week! Thanks for making this great connection with the Bishop Family!*

Birthday Cards are a great way to acknowledge someone's special day, and I feel that teachers are great at celebrating our students and making them feel special in ways that are meaningful to them. Teachers are very skilled at knowing which students would feel embarrassed at a whole-class singing of the birthday song, and would instead prefer a quick high five and a pencil. Giving kids the options for how (or *if*) they'd like to celebrate their day is a beautiful and responsive way to celebrate our students and honor their preferences.

Most teachers acknowledge students' birthdays. A great way to connect with families is to send home a birthday card to parents, siblings, aunts/uncles/grandparents/neighbors —whoever lives at home. This is such a positive surprise when a mom receives snail mail addressed to her to celebrate her birthday from her child's teacher. I can guarantee you'd be among the first teachers to ever do this! Perhaps this doesn't seem very plausible if you have a large class, or if you teach middle school or high school. Get together with your team or school leaders and discuss if this is something you'd like to do together!

<u>Acknowledging Celebrations, Holidays, Milestones, & Special Moments</u> of our families is another way to have a positive interaction. If a student's sibling is participating in a special service at their house of faith, send them a card to congratulate them, wish them luck, or share your pride. Keep it short and simple and sign your name. If there is a cultural holiday that a family is celebrating, send a special note.

<u>The Birth of a Sibling or Family Member at Home</u> is very special indeed. Slip a $5 Target gift card or a travel pack of diapers into your student's backpack to send home. Again, we are working on teacher's salaries here, so small amounts or a simple card still goes a long way in building a relationship!

<u>Student Selfies</u> is an idea that we discussed in a previous chapter, but doing this not only builds up a student's confidence as a learner, it also helps connect the adults at home to the learning at school. When I get that text message as a parent from my child's teacher that says, "WOW—TJ rocked his math assignment yesterday" along with a picture of him happy at school… that means a lot to me as a parent. Not only does it make me feel proud of my son, but it also makes me feel that his teacher loves him and is proud of him, too.

THE COMPLIMENT SANDWICH THAT NO ONE ORDERED

When I was taking education classes for my undergraduate degree, I learned about the infamous "compliment sandwich". This was delivered to pre-service teachers as THE WORLD'S GREATEST

STRATEGY for delivering bad news to parents. Perhaps you've heard of this sandwich before, or perhaps you've been force-fed one as a parent. It's like this: when you have a piece of bad news to share about a student, you put it in the middle of two (often very unrelated) compliments to "soften the blow." For example:

Teacher: I just wanted to tell you how helpful David has been lately.

Parent: *thinking this will be a very positive conference, smiles*

Teacher: But, we've had a lot of problems with his behavior. He's been getting into a lot of fights on the playground for the past two weeks, and he's lost a few privileges. We wrote up a plan that we'd like you to sign.

Parent: *thinking, Woah, this took a turn. Frowns*

Teacher: Thanks so much for signing this. We know David will turn things around. Did I tell you he got an A on his math test last week?

Parent: *confused, thinking are things going well or are they not going well?*

When we are compliment-sandwiching our parents, it can often send very mixed messages and leave parents confused about their child's progress and development.

It's also often a bologna sandwich—as in, *phony bologna*. When the three statements/compliments/problems are unrelated, you look like you're all over the place and parents don't know if you like their kid or not. I've never gone to a diner and overheard anyone order a bologna sandwich. No one orders that. Don't force-feed those to parents, especially if you've already provided a healthy diet of ongoing positive communication along with an active relationship. Save the compliment sandwiches for your cheat day when you binge on Oreos. A cookie sandwich is much more enjoyable, anyway.

THE PHONE CALLS YOU NEVER WANT TO MAKE & THE MEETINGS YOU NEVER WANT TO HAVE

Yes, there will be times where you have to call home and deliver bad news to parents. Perhaps there was a fight at school or a piece of missing work, or there are other concerns of some sort. It's best to be direct, especially if you're asking the parent or guardian to come in for a meeting. It is not fair to blindside them. Consider your language and ensure it seems inviting. Does the following invitation seem inviting? What might you change or add?

> "Mrs. Spina, we would like for you to come in so we can all brainstorm ways to support TJ with his behavior. We can all share some thoughts and ideas and create a plan together. Please let us know when a good time is for us to come together. For this meeting, we'll be in the conference room towards the front of the school, and I invited the social worker and our Assistant Principal to be a part of our brainstorming meeting so that we can all bring forward some great ideas. We want to hear your ideas, too, since he's your son and you know him best. You can offer some great insight for us!"

When the parent arrives at school, offer them some water and a comfortable chair. Be mindful of how many adults are at this meeting, because that can be incredibly intimidating for any parent. Letting the parent know in advance that other team members will be there will also ensure that you are not violating anyone's trust or expectation. Also, if all your interactions have taken place in your classroom, but this next meeting is going to be held in a conference room or the principal's office, it can throw off the energy and can unintentionally destroy trust. Be sure an interpreter is present to provide language access for families who need it. Introduce each member of the team (if there is a team) around the table.

I'll also note that when we *only* make contact with the home for bad news (especially when there's no established relationship, to begin with), this destroys relationships. This gets harder as the students get older, especially if the parent has had bad experiences with teachers in the past, or if they had bad experiences with teachers when they were a student.

No matter what you may say, the parents may hear a message of defeat. Here are a few examples:

What the teacher says	What the parent hears
Your child isn't doing any homework.	You're failing as a parent.
Your child isn't behaving in class.	You're failing as a parent.
Your child is making bad choices.	You're failing as a parent.
Your child is failing three classes.	You're failing as a parent.
Your child is being disrespectful to others.	You're failing as a parent.

As a human being, if my phone rang from a certain phone number that only delivered bad news to me, I simply wouldn't answer the phone. Honestly. I would let it go to voicemail and I would not return that call. Would you?

NOTITAS EN MI ALMOHADA/NOTES ON MY PILLOW

Most of the families I serve work outside the home. For many families, their work hours don't always align with the hours that the children are home from school. I've had kids over the years who stay up late because they want to see their mom after she's done working a late shift. I've had kids who only see one of their parents or guardians on the weekend because their work/school schedules don't align.

Knowing that about our families is important. We also know that certain pieces of paper still need to be signed, like field trip slips.

One day, during a parent-teacher conference, I was discussing this very thing with a mom and her son. He stayed up late at night to have a snack with her when she got home from work. As a mom, I get it, and advice from my mouth should never come between that special time between a mother and her son. We talked about ways that he could be sure that his body is getting adequate rest so that he can be successful at school and home. We all thought it was a good idea for him to take a brief nap after getting home from school before doing his homework and helping his grandma with dinner. It worked out perfectly.

During that same conference, we talked about ways to ensure that school communication was getting to the mom. We all left the meeting with a plan to hang stuff on the refrigerator with a magnet they borrowed from my whiteboard. We tried it for a week or two and decided it wasn't working.

I asked mom about space in her bedroom. Many times when she comes home from work, she walks right in and goes right to sleep. She suggested that they try placing notes on her pillow and then talked to her son about the new plan. It worked beautifully. It was such a success that on the days where he didn't have any papers to put on her pillow, he'd write her a sweet note or draw her a picture. She then started to do the same thing to him to see if he'd be okay with a note from mom instead of staying up late. Over the next few weeks and months, he'd go to bed with the note, and other times he'd stay up late to spend quality time with her. I thought this was beautiful.

I asked the mom and son if I could share their idea with other families because it could help other families who had the same type of work schedule. Mom laughed and said sure! From then on, that was information I shared with families during our first parent evening together.

USING AN INTERPRETER

Set the norms at the beginning of any meeting that involves the use of the linguistic talents of an interpreter:

> "Thank you all for coming to our meeting today. We will first go ahead and give introductions around the table…. Great, thanks, everyone. Now that we know who's who, let's talk about ways for all of us to communicate effectively with our interpreter that we are so glad has joined us today. When we have a message to convey to parents, we will talk directly to the parent, not the interpreter. That means we will face the parent and look at the parent while we speak. We will also speak in chunks because that will allow the interpreter time to share the message so that nothing gets lost or left out. I know some of the teachers have prepared a few items on a notecard that they wanted to be sure were mentioned today, so they may pass that notecard to the interpreter while they are talking, as that may help with interpretation. Mrs. Paul, thank you for being our inter-

preter today. If at any point, you need us to pause or repeat anything, just let us know—we are happy to do that. Parents, if you would like for us to slow down or take a break, please let us know, too."

Teachers, parents, and the interpreter may feel a little less awkward about where to look and who to speak to while sharing information, and this only takes a few minutes to ensure that everyone knows the expectation.

MOVING BEYOND VIA REFLECTION & ACTION

Share out your reflections & action steps on Twitter using #MovingBeyondEdu

REFLECT:

- How do you prefer to communicate at work? With your friends? With your family members?
- What platforms do you typically use to communicate with families? What has worked in the past and what hasn't worked? Why?

ACT:

How do you find out the communication preferences of the families you serve? Below, create a communications survey and include options for families:

I like to hear from <u>the teacher</u> by...	I like to hear from <u>the school</u> by...
☐ Seesaw, Schoology, or similar platform	☐ Seesaw, Schoology, or similar platform
☐ Phone Call	☐ Phone Call
☐ Text message	☐ Text message
☐ Video announcement (YouTube link)	☐ Video announcement (YouTube link)
☐ Social Media (Facebook? Instagram? Twitter?)	☐ Social Media (Facebook? Instagram? Twitter?)
☐ Email	☐ Email
☐ Postal mail	☐ Postal mail

- How can you divide and conquer communications methods on your team?

Method	Teammate who can create post/content:
Seesaw/Schoology post	
Phone Call (or phone blast)	
Text Message (or text blast)	
Video Announcement	
Social Media posts (words, graphics, etc)	
Email message	
Postal Letter/Flyer	

- How do you express to families that you are their teammate? Make your own list below of reasons why your families may wish to reach out to you or to the school!

Reasons You Might Reach Out to Me:	Reasons You Might Reach Out to the School:

10

BEYOND YOUR CALL TO SERVE

REMEMBERING YOURSELF

I have been avoiding writing this chapter. This has been on my heart for years, but I have been putting this off for several reasons. I know this chapter will make my parents mad. It's going to put me through a lot of shame, guilt, and disappointment in myself. However, I believe I need to tell this story because I feel that many of us educators are in these same situations. I want to tell you that I hear you, I see you, and I'm here for you.

I am the youngest of three daughters. My sisters are wonderful human beings who inspire me. They work hard in all they do. They are both devoted, loving mothers to their children. They look for opportunities to serve others. They are my best friends in the world. As the baby of my family, I've always wanted to prove myself—that I can do hard things. I can do things independently, without asking for help. I guess I still behave like this in many situations, but I'm working on it.

When I was early in my career, I was very guilty of this. I wanted to serve, lead, support, and do big things for my students and their families well beyond the classroom doors.

There was also a lot going on in my personal and professional life. During my first year of teaching, I got married to my husband. During my second year of teaching, I gave birth to my son when I was 23 years old. I was young, and I didn't make a lot of money. Neither did my husband, who was just getting started in his career as a civil engineer. I want to be very clear here—my son was not an accident. To this day I tell my kids that Mommy and Daddy couldn't wait a single second more to have a baby. While we weren't planning on becoming parents just 11 months after our wedding, we felt blessed beyond measure and we were determined to give him the best that we could.

I was desperate to serve kids and families and I felt eager to do it all. My teammates and I launched a tutoring program for our students who were striving in reading. At the same time, we also launched a parent program for our Hispanic families that offered workshops in Spanish, along with free childcare and free transportation. There was a lot of energy and enthusiasm, and it was a time I'll be forever grateful to have had.

However, my district also was still in the stage of freezing salaries within a certain number of years to encourage teachers to pursue their master's degrees. I couldn't quit my job and I needed more money. Bills were piling up. I had awful guilt for not being ready to be a mama, and I searched all around for a daycare that we felt comfortable sending him, knowing that we'd both be working... a lot. We needed to cover all our bills plus his daycare tuition, which was outrageously expensive, so I enrolled in my master's degree program and started taking night classes each Tuesday night.

The days and nights were hard. I was fighting for every minute I had with my son. I felt like I never saw him, though. I needed the money from tutoring. I often dropped him off early at daycare, where he was usually one of the first kids there. Then after working all day, I stayed after school several days of the week to tutor students. I'd race to him after tutoring, eager to soak up time together. He'd be so exhausted from all the stimulation at daycare that he'd usually go to bed early. I'd cry putting him to bed most nights.

Each Tuesday, I'd race from school to daycare to my parents' house, where my husband would meet me to pick up our son. I'd drive to night class, where I'd sit for four hours, trying to concentrate, but mostly wishing for more time with my son. Nights and weekends were spent doing school work, doing homework for my classes, or reporting data for our tutoring program and parent program.

I wanted so desperately to serve the families I supported for our parent program. Like me, the parents loved their children so much and wanted to do anything they could to give their children the best opportunities possible. I felt connected to them, not only as their teacher but as a fellow parent. I understood their dreams for their kids. I respected them, and I felt a true partnership. We could truly move mountains for their kids, together as a team!

On some nights of our parent workshops, I'd ask my husband to attend and bring our son along. While we couldn't be next to each other, knowing that we could be in the same room brought me comfort. They'd sit together in the back of the school library, on the floor, reading books or eating Cheerios. Now and then, my son would toddle up to me as I stood at the microphone, and he'd hug my ankles. At first, I was worried that my principal at the time would frown at this, but he was a true family man, and he understood my need to feel connected to my son. The moms would laugh, my son would run back down the rows of chairs to my husband, and the show would go on. The moms would take turns picking him up, giving him *besitos,* or handing him a cookie.

Some nights were harder than others, but I was determined to "hustle hard" and "be strong" and not let anyone know just how much I was struggling emotionally, physically, financially, and spiritually. Bills piled up and credit cards started to max out, but I was determined to be the best mama and provider I could be.

On certain nights, my husband would have to travel, work late, or attend events. Remember, he was also early in his career and was eager to do well. We both were doggy-paddling our way through life.

One night, I had to do my race from school, to tutoring, to daycare, and back to school for a parent event. My son would come with me, but my husband was working late. I knew it would be a late night, so I threw a few extra snacks in the diaper bag that morning. I figured that we could stop at a drive-through that evening after the event was over.

Because my teammates were so amazing, the evening went smoothly as always. Parents packed the library for parent learning, and their kids had wonderful activities to do in the gym. At the end of the evening, my son grew fussy as we cleaned up. I picked him up and knew that he was hungry and we had gone through all of the snacks I had packed, so I thanked my teammates, and we headed out.

I got to the McDonalds parking lot, and I checked the clock. It had gotten late. I felt so incredibly guilty as my son now cried. I felt like a terrible mother. I tried to play his favorite music to calm him, but I knew it wasn't going to work. I pulled up to the drive-through ordering screen, placed our order, and pulled around to go and pay. The cashier read the total, and I grabbed my wallet. I froze.

At my school, our cafeteria staff would place notices in teachers' mailboxes for them to distribute to parents in their "take-home folders." Normally the notices would give parents a heads-up that their lunch balances were running low. There were a few particular families that had fallen on hard times, and while they hadn't qualified for Free/Reduced meals at one point, we knew that they would soon.

I had gotten reprimanded a time or two when I tried to write checks to cover the balance of lunch cards. My name was on it, so it was easy to see that it was me paying and not a family. Instead of asking why, I was told to "stay in my lane" and not "enable families," I tried to push back against this one person telling me that, but I quickly realized it wasn't going to be a battle I was going to win, so I'd just cover the family with cash instead. I'd place the bills in an empty envelope and I would walk it down to the cafeteria, saying that the family just turned it in.

Well, earlier that same day, I noticed that one of the notices was back and that the family had owed the school money. I grabbed the note, went to my classroom and pulled out my cash, and walked it down to turn it in. I didn't think anything of it.

But now, my son was in the backseat crying. I had no more cash in my wallet. I knew my credit cards would get declined, but I handed two of them to the cashier, praying with all I had that they would miraculously go through this time. They were both declined. Cars behind me grew impatient, so I apologized to the cashier as my son screamed in the backseat.

I pulled under a streetlight in the parking lot and debated what to do. I felt around the bottom of my purse, the diaper bag, and looked under car seats. I had enough change to cover the cost of his Happy Meal. Tears streamed down my cheeks as I tried to sing songs to my son. I got back in the car, drove back around, and paid for his meal in coins.

I watched him eat in the car. His cheeks were red and his eyes were puffy from crying. I turned up his music a little louder, thankful that he had enough.

Tears ran down my face and I tried to stifle my crying with my hands. I didn't want him to hear me. He ate his dinner in his car seat. I couldn't bring myself to drive home yet. I felt like a complete failure.

We eventually made it home, put on his jammies, and did his bedtime routine. As I put him to bed and closed his door, I sat on the floor with my head in my hands as a million emotions poured through me.

Was this what it meant to serve?

Let me be very clear: This was not okay. I know this *now*. I understand this *today*. I know there are a million sayings about not pouring from an empty cup, or about putting on your oxygen mask before helping others. I've posted some of those quotes and messages before on my social media feeds and I've found some mediocre levels of comfort from them over the years. However, why does it take experiences like mine to be pushed too far for us to learn this lesson for ourselves?

Our own families have to come first. Adam Welcome shared this message at the end of his keynote at the Teach Better Conference in 2019. At the end of his keynote, while people were clapping their hands, I sat glued to my chair. I felt my face reddening. I felt the tears coming. I put my hand over my mouth but felt my shoulders shaking as I cried. I knew my makeup would be a mess. I knew I'd get looks. (I didn't... the folks at that conference were not the judging kind.) I felt embarrassed to be so overcome with emotion, thinking back to that night almost 10 years ago in the McDonalds parking lot under the street light.

I can say with 100% confidence that after reading this, my parents will be calling me. They will be so upset to hear that I didn't ask for help. They will say that I should have just called them and they would have fed both my son and me that night. My sisters will likely do the same thing and have the same reaction.

I want you to know that this story brings me so much shame

as a mother. I've maybe told four people this story. It's a moment I am not proud of but one I feel that I need to share. So many of us are pushed into giving and serving beyond our means… because there is so much need. We hear stories of our students and our families that shatter our hearts, put things in perspective, and help us realize how blessed we are.

Yet we have to serve within limits.

Our time with our families is precious. I felt like I fought for every minute with my son, but I also felt so strongly called to serve my students and families. I stretched out so much of my time in the classroom, at tutoring sessions, or parent events. I could have easily told my teammates that I needed more time at home, but I didn't. I wanted to serve and support, but I was sacrificing precious time that I won't ever get back.

My son is now 13. I'm sure eventually he'll see this or hear about it at some point. I've been too embarrassed to share this, post it, or even talk about it. If his ears ever catch wind of this, it is my hope and prayer that he knows how much I love him and his sister and that I've learned a lot of hard lessons over the years of being a parent. I do mess up (daily), but I hope he knows that I will always put him and our family first. I hope he learns that it is good to serve but to first take care of himself. I pray that my kids will have a better balance than I feel that I didn't yet have back then.

Knowing there is great need weighs heavy on most of us. We lose sleep at night over our kids and other people's kids. We worry about our families that we support. We want to do so much.

Educators have so much passion in their hearts. If you are leading in your system as a lone change agent or disruptor, I know the weight feels heavy on your shoulders. You may be feeling that if you don't take charge of something or say some-thing or do something, no one else will. You may feel that if you don't take on this program or initiate that change, then it simply won't happen.

Sometimes I look at the systems I serve and I feel overwhelmed. I feel frustrated by the lack of equity that still exists. I feel down on myself or my work because things still aren't where I feel like they should be. *My goodness!* I'll say to myself. *It's 2021 and we're still doing xyz?* I know I'm not the only one. Maybe you've said this, too.

We have to remember that change takes time. We have to remember that this is a marathon, not a sprint. We have to remember to be good to ourselves along the way.

On the days where I feel frustrated, overwhelmed, or defeated, I'm not in any mood to revisit my Why, although that's what I'm told to do by many books and blogs. For me, I know when I'm feeling defeated, I need to pause altogether.

I am glad that adult social-emotional learning has gotten so much attention lately because while we stress all of the ways to support the social-emotional development of the children we serve and support, we rarely reflect on the ways we are teaching ourselves about self-care, mindfulness, or emotional intelligence.

My friend Dorina Sackman Ebuwa (follow her on Twitter @Dorina_BELIEVE) has an incredible YouTube series called #BELIEVE_Cafe and I highly recommend it to all educators. She talks to the viewer through episodes of transformative emotional intelligence and shows a lot of vulnerability as she shares her feelings and walks us through each part of the journey. I'm thankful to her for this, as I'm learning an awful lot about myself and emotional intelligence.

Self-care isn't about spas and manicures. It's not about walks through fields of daisies, bubble baths, or massages. It's personal to you. Maybe it's crying it out. It could be going to bed early. Perhaps it's wearing the colors that bring you joy, reading a favorite book for 10 minutes, or popping on a TV show that makes you laugh. I love what Mandy Froehlich said recently in a Facebook Live—*it's about being more intentional with my time.*

I have been guilty of letting things build up over time until finally, I burst into tears at a team meeting. I remember once this happened and my 3rd-grade teammates listened to me and comforted me, telling me that they wanted to help, and I didn't have to do anything alone. *I wish I had asked for help sooner.*

Years go on and you learn and grow from your experiences. I know that sometimes, I have to decline family events at night. I have to go home to my family. I know that sometimes, I have to say no to being on that committee because I can't possibly fit one more puzzle piece into my day. I know that sometimes, I have to just say no.

Investing in yourself is critical. You are important, you are worthy, and you are on a mission. You're in this for the long haul. We must set limits and boundaries, and stick to them. Don't link your email to your cell phone. Don't check your work email after 6 pm (*or 4 pm!*—do what makes sense to you!). If you must work over the weekend, set aside a block of time to get work done, but set that time limit and hold firm to it. Don't work outside of that block. Your weekend is for you. Rest, recharge, refuel and relax. Your work can wait for another day.

Be mindful of your body, your spirit, your mind. Note how your body feels and changes and sits differently when you're in a room with certain people. Be intentional with your commute. Do something that rests your soul, soothes your spirit, or inspires your mind, like listening to a fun podcast or playing the music of your faith. Say no without guilt trips. Meditate. Do yoga. Play with stickers. Give yourself a "bubble break" with a strip of bubble wrap.

In conversation, many times folks will ask me if I've seen a certain movie or show. About 99% of the time, I haven't, and it used to be something I found so embarrassing about myself. I never know what the cool shows are, and even the biggest movies that everyone's seen, I probably haven't. People would giggle with me and I'd joke that I live under a rock. The truth is, I don't find joy in television and movies. Sitting down for long periods makes me anxious. I prefer reading books (not e-books) and I love "fluffy" books if I'm not doing some professional reading.

My joy comes in the form of wearing bright colors (I'm in neon colors pretty much year-round) and being around bright colors. I enjoy getting dressed up for absolutely no reason. I love decorating my planner with fun stickers that help me feel motivated and organized. My delight comes in doing Facebook Lives with my daughter about our current foster puppies, watching her transform into a rescue advocate while she cuddles up close with a sweet little pup. I enjoy watching fashion bloggers on Instagram Stories doing try-ons of cute and affordable clothing. I love to make lists and decorate my townhouse and I *really* love to go shopping.

You deserve that "time off" where you are not dedicating your time to serving others. You must serve yourself.

I'm here to tell you that it is a heavy weight to carry alone, and you must have a network. You must have a system of support that you can turn to.

MOVING BEYOND VIA REFLECTION & ACTION

Share out your reflections & action steps on Twitter using #MovingBeyondEdu

REFLECT:

- When have you reached a breaking point? What led up to it? What got you through it? What did you learn from that experience?
- What brings you joy outside of your job?

ACT:

- What do you do when you feel yourself reaching your limit? Make an action plan that includes identifying something to remove from your plate, investing in yourself, and asking for help.

When I need to PAUSE, I can...	1. 2. 3.
Things I can remove from my plate or revisit later:	1. 2. 3.
People I can go to for encouragement or support:	1. 2. 3.

- What would you do FOR YOURSELF if you had an extra 5 minutes, 15 minutes, or 30 minutes in your schedule?

If I had an extra 5 minutes for myself, I would...	If I had an extra 15 minutes for myself, I would...	If I had an extra 15 minutes for myself, I would...
1.	1.	1.
2.	2,	2.
3.	3.	3.

- Now highlight one activity from each category and see how you can intentionally plug each into your schedule this week!

BEYOND OUR SCHOOL WALLS

BEING A COMMUNITY CONNECTOR

*W*e have discussed the importance of building up our students, our parents, and our schools. Now let's move beyond the walls of our classrooms and buildings. How do we build up our community of supports so that we can remember we are never alone in our quest to make a difference?

We need to be informed educators not only of what's best practice in terms of instruction, assessment, and social-emotional development, but what's also of what's available in the communities we serve.

No matter how many years you've served in your community, you may not know the entire scope of what's out there. No matter how many years our families have lived in our communities, they may not know of great resources that could benefit them or someone they know. Things change all the time. Many social service agencies will share that one of their biggest challenges is getting the word out about what services and supports are available to families.

A friend of mine, Jill Brickman, is a woman whom I deeply

respect and admire. For many years, she was the director of our local food pantry that serves many of the families in my school district. She and I have spoken about the difficulty in keeping all local leaders informed of changes that were results of a grant being approved recently, a new partnership formed, or an influx of donations. Things change constantly! If we aren't able to speak to the masses about all of these changes, that could mean that a needed resource isn't connected to a family in need. This means that educators need to be connected and informed.

A few short years ago, I found out that a new connection had been made in the community between a church and an auto body shop. A terrible thing can happen to families who are living on or near the poverty line—if the family car breaks down, the parent cannot get to work. In the suburbs or rural communities, while there are buses, it is more difficult to get around. If the parent cannot get to work, they cannot pay their bills. It is a quick and scary domino effect that can create homelessness in just weeks.

There was a mechanic who belonged to the church and was willing to support families in need by providing his auto services free of charge. Families would only need to pay for parts. When I heard about this, I was so excited to run back to my school district and tell our school social workers. They were instantly able to think of a few families who could benefit from this.

Very often, all it takes is one community connection that can open the door to lots of other opportunities and resources for families. For example, at certain food pantries, other events take place throughout the year that pantry clients can partake in like a free holiday event or even a school supply drive. Social service agencies are often connected by a network to other agencies that they can seek out when they're unable to meet a specific need for a family. This is why it's critically important that our families are connected.

I don't know about you, but paperwork of any kind intimidates me. Honestly. It doesn't matter where I go, if you hand me a clipboard with a stack of papers to fill out, I will get itchy. I'm afraid of writing the wrong thing on the wrong line, making a spelling mistake, or even writing the wrong answer. It just makes me nervous! Remember, I have a linguistic privilege as an English-speaker in the US. I also have the privilege of being literate (yes, it's a privilege). Can you imagine how much more intimidating forms might be for those who don't have the same privileges as me?

With immigration policy changing often and with new rules, it is important that our families feel informed and can have their questions answered by someone who speaks their language when they are filling out any paperwork for aid. While schools and school personnel can never offer any legal advice to families, we can at least connect them to agencies that can support them with this. Sometimes, it helps just to be a friendly face at the agency to offer a smile and sit with them while they fill out paperwork.

Being present at the agency can offer a sense of relief or comfort in recognizing a familiar face. It can provide a sense of comfort or relief when they're trying to navigate a new situation. It can also allow introductions to be made with folks who are at the agency. If my presence can help facilitate a partnership or support that can benefit the family, I have no problem meeting families after work every once in a while.

I love being able to see the families I serve out in the community. I enjoy being able to connect with others through my language skills if I'm interpreting for an event. I find joy in giving out hugs and high-fives to the kids I know at the events that I volunteer at and I love meeting siblings and other family members.

Each year near the holidays, I serve as an interpreter for families at a beautiful event that is a partnership between a local history center and our food pantry. I join families as they walk through a forest with lanterns, listen to a holiday story, complete an art project, and later meet Santa Claus. This is one of my favorite events of the year because it is so family-focused. I see the moms snuggle up to their babies. I see the dads lift their kids high over their heads to try to spot an owl in the trees. I watch as the little ones jump up and down upon hearing Santa's footsteps. I giggle with the adults as the kids decorate holiday cookies and drink hot cocoa. I enjoy this so much because while I'm present at school as we talk about academics and homework completion, I also need to be with families in moments like these where we are simply enjoying each other's company and sharing in a wonderful, positive experience together.

Sounds magical, right? It is. So, how do we get started? I wish I could tell you that I have the secret sauce or a very specific and specialized process, but the truth is, you can Google it or just use your social media feeds to find everything you want to know. You can search for youth-centered organizations in the town you serve or in the towns nearby. Go ahead and slide into their DMs (wow, is that phrase really inside of an education book?). Introduce yourself, ask some questions, and see what they're all about. You can even ask for a tour of their facility or a meeting with a director or a staff member. Offer to volunteer at their next event so you can see the ways they serve firsthand and meet other folks who are trying to make a difference.

The purpose of social media is to be a connection. Not only to friends and family (or students and their families) but also to our communities. It is easier and faster for agencies and organizations to make a quick post or update instead of modifying their entire website to make an announcement. Go ahead and "like" and follow those agencies, and be sure to turn on notifications so that you can be alerted when there's an update. You'll have firsthand knowledge of the latest events, opportunities, programs, and resources that you can then share with your families and your colleagues.

If you're still not into that idea, keep it simple and use your phone to make phone call introductions. Do some light research about the organization in advance and write down specific questions you have. Questions may include inquiries about fees for services, scholarships, etc.

As we are branching out in the communities we serve, it's important to consider volunteering for organizations that speak to our passions and interests. For me, I volunteer as a foster for puppies! I have met so many wonderful rescue folks over the last five years. I have opportunities to connect with people who are in my rescue organization's foster and volunteer network. I also have had the chance to meet folks from other rescues at different adoption events. I've had great conversations with potential adopters and families, some of whom I still keep in contact with, even if they never ended up adopting one of our dogs. As time has passed, it has been wonderful to build relationships and broaden my circle. I have met so many folks that are like-minded and have a desire to serve others and make a difference. Many of my rescue buddies were right there when I had a plea for more snacks for my classroom, gym shoes for a student, or even socks for our clean sock bin that I kept in the classroom.

These animal lovers have become my friends. I know their kids' names and spouses. They've introduced me to their friends. They have donated books, socks, shoelaces, healthy snacks, business cards, and more to my classroom over the years. They've shared my pleas for donations on their social media pages. Friends-of-friends have supported my kids without ever stepping foot into our school.

Doing this has humbled me in so many ways. There was one school year where I had a particularly needy class. The poverty was unlike any other group I had previously had. I was funneling money into my students and families. *We've all done this at some point*—purchased clothing, gym shoes, snow pants, winter boots, mittens, healthy snacks, school supplies, even cover the costs of local team sports so that the kids can participate. While this is nice —*this is costly*. If you are running on an empty wallet, to begin with, you must know your limits. We all talk about being cautious of pouring from an empty cup, but we rarely talk about this from a financial lens. You cannot offer or share financial support from an empty wallet.

Try your best, make connections, expand your circle, give back. We all want to make a difference, but we need to do it together—not alone! And by all means… continue to practice sincere gratitude for those who are helping you, your students, and your families along the way.

YOUTH AGENCIES

Other resources that you may wish to tap into include local youth organizations. If your town doesn't have an agency, perhaps the town next door does. See what types of programs are available and what the costs are to participate (if any). Ask about scholarships or sliding scales.

Folks in my school district have developed a strong relationship with a youth organization in the town I serve. Years ago, we were lucky enough to combine resources for a summer project that began as just an idea. Over the years, the program has changed up a bit, but the ultimate goal is to provide a fun and safe space for kids to learn, grow, and smile. The program allows students a fun summer experience two days per week in the summer where they can receive a meal (provided by local churches), take a field trip, and participate in STEM or service-learning opportunities. Our schools brought teachers and they brought case managers. We all brought volunteers. We shared space and transportation costs. This program is now in its 4th year and expanding to support multiple schools in our district.

HOUSES OF FAITH

As someone who grew up attending church in my Sunday best (including the itchiest tights known to humanity), and with my momma as the youth pastor and later, associate pastor, I grew to recognize that houses of faith are good places to be if you want to find folks with a servant's heart. Regardless of what type of faith, religion, or denomination—regardless of if the folks attend a church, a synagogue, or a mosque—some people want to serve and help others.

Remember the summer program I shared. Our local faith communities (almost a dozen different ones!) provided bagged lunches for our students so that they would have a meal during the summer before taking a field trip. In turn, the students made fun thank you cards for those groups. What a wonderful support system we have available to us if we look around!

One year I was able to collect about 20 pumpkins from a house of faith a few towns over who was willing to donate them to my class. Each year, they hosted a pumpkin farm on their grounds as a fundraiser. I checked in with parents before picking them up, because not every family celebrates Halloween, and pumpkins are typically a Halloween-related activity. We were able to paint *calaveras* on our pumpkins with white paint and colorful Sharpie markers, which combined one tradition (Halloween) with another tradition (Día de los Muertos—which again, not everyone celebrates). The students loved being able to combine two cultures into one project and made beautiful projects to take home to their families. We shared photos with the church so they could see our beautiful artwork that represents a melding of two cultures. They replied that they absolutely loved them and that I should come back next year for more pumpkins for next year's class.

During the pandemic where food insecurity rose to the forefront of many minds and hearts, I reached out to a local church and explained the need. Weeks later, they offered all families in the community a pop-up drive-through pantry!

LOCAL BUSINESSES

I've shared the way my students loved creating resumes and business cards. It was so helpful for me to broaden my network and email or call local businesses to "befriend" them: ask them questions, request photos of their work, or invite them to share words of wisdom with third graders in their neighborhood.

Even if we don't have a direct question for them, it can certainly build up a community to send them a hand-drawn picture via snail mail for them to hang up in their business. This led to lots of fun messages thanking us for sending them a smile. Who wouldn't like getting a sweet picture in the mail within your stack of bills?

One year in late November, a thick envelope appeared in my school mailbox. It wasn't stamped, so someone must have come by the school to drop it off. The handwriting sprawled across said that this package came "directly from the North Pole." My interest was piqued for sure. I asked my front office who it was from, and they smiled and said they weren't sure. I thought perhaps it was them, but they shook their heads no. I went back to the classroom with the envelope and took a picture. I always took pictures of exciting mail we received and sent them to my husband or my sisters or parents. I told them all that we got a package from the North Pole.

I will say here that 100% of my students celebrated Christmas. This I knew for a fact. I typically will ask parents at the beginning of the school year what holidays they celebrate, avoid, and even the way they celebrate birthdays (or don't!). It makes me cringe the way we center Christmas in public schools, but I digress.

While my students were still at recess, I cracked the package open on the edge. I didn't want to open the package in front of the student without knowing what was in there first. What I saw took my breath away. I waited for the kids to come back from recess.

We sat down and I put the envelope in front of them without saying a word. Eyes got wide. Jaws dropped. Silence. They looked around at each other. They knew that wasn't my handwriting. This must be something special, something magical.

I opened the package and inside was a $25 Kohl's gift card for *every single child in my classroom*. The class was overjoyed! A note inside said Merry Christmas! I couldn't believe someone dropped this off for them, without even leaving a note. I wondered who this was from. As kids were celebrating their gift card surprises, what happened next touched me in my soul.

The kids immediately started listing what they would buy for their families. One little girl shared that she was going to purchase socks for her baby brother. One boy shared that he was going to buy his mom a necklace. Another girl said she would get her big sister a 3-pack of her favorite lipgloss. Not one child said they were going to purchase something for themselves.

Later on, I found out who my secret Santa was... it was a small business owner who had an auto glass shop about 30 minutes away from my school. His name is Jerry Nemeth, a man whose business had been struggling for some time. He was in no financial position to give at that time, but he did anyway. While bills stacked up, he wanted to bless others, and he immediately thought of the amazing children that were in Room 9. Jerry is a good man, and I'm so proud to call him my dad.

KNOW YOUR CIRCLE

Utilize your already existing network of the people you know and love. Do your friends have a special message of inspiration or a talent or gift that could expose your students to a neat skillset? I reached out to friends that I grew up with who are in the music industry. If you are familiar with house music in the late 90s, you probably have heard of Pamp & Da Knox. Rafael Rodriguez (aka Pamp) and his brother Danny (of Drummond Brothers) came to visit my third graders to share how to use creativity to produce a message and express yourself. They shared examples of art, music, sound, written word, graphic design, and more. The students connected to them immediately, because they showed them real-life examples of music and art they love and that they see in their own neighborhoods. We talked about the importance of knowing your culture and language (they are Puerto Rican) and how you can always incorporate your identity into your craft.

The students loved seeing how to make music and they were so excited to see some of the pieces of recording equipment brought in. Then, Rafe and Danny asked the kids what their interests were —what were they passionate about? The kids exploded with excitement as they shared that we just got a classroom drone and we love flying it around once it is charged. Then they asked the students what they did to stay motivated on bad days. The kids were excited to share their mantra with them.

Well it turns out, Rafe and Danny had a few things up their sleeves after spending time with us. They reached out to their friends at Durty Laundry (a clothing line based out of Texas) and had them create a custom t-shirt for every student with our school logo as well as our mantra. It didn't stop there! They also hit up *their* network of friends and family and asked for a sponsor for each child to purchase every single student a drone of their very own. I'll never forget the day that Rafe and Danny came back to visit us with these amazing surprises. The kids were jumping up and down with excitement and I couldn't stop crying. I'll never forget how emotional I felt, thinking of how many folks were in my students' corner and wanted to give them such a special gift that they could share with their families.

SPREADING SMILES

We tried to practice random acts of kindness throughout the year. This became a favorite activity because you could feel all of the positive energy. It taught us to actively look for ways to support other people.

We thanked our bus drivers at random times throughout the year with cards, posters, and one time, a balloon. (We did a balloon one year and we were politely asked to not do that again, oops!)

After a group of kids saw a commercial about someone passing out flowers, the kids asked if we could do that. So the next day, I stopped to pick up some flowers, and we walked around the school handing them out to teachers.

Another time, we wrote positive messages of love, care, and support, and we carefully went out into the staff parking lot. While the kids watched, I carefully placed the notes on the windshields of teachers' cars. We had a ton of positive feedback from teachers who said that it brightened up their day!

We sent holiday cards to local nursing homes, as well as our fire department, police department, local businesses, and different agencies. We invited the other classrooms in our school to join us in our efforts.

We loved looking for ways to spread joy and kindness.

KEEP YOUR EYES OPEN

Anytime I went to my public library, I'd grab a few of the local Spanish newspapers that were free. It was important that my students saw their language out in the community. Sometimes there were great stories that I'd share with the kids, or posters that we'd hang up in the room. There were articles that I'd share with families or things I'd clip out and share with a particular mom.

One time my eyes fell on a coloring contest. I made a copy of the sheet and sent it home with families, in case they wanted their kids to enter it. I even sent home a stamped and addressed envelope so they could mail it in—but again, they were the parents, and they could decide whether or not to enter the contest. Several students entered.

Weeks went by and one day, one of my students burst into the classroom door and yelled, "Maestra, I won! I won!" It turns out, she won $250 for her work. She told me the whole family celebrated and planned on going out for dinner together that weekend.

DREAM BIG, DREAM TOGETHER

As you branch out and broaden your support network, make friends. As you meet folks or attend events or meetings, stay after to talk and hang out. Get to know the people. Celebrate their accomplishments and show your support for their work. Ask about their families and their passions. And always, always dream together. Dream out loud, share your ideas, even if they seem too big or too wild. You just never know who could help you make that dream a reality. Our kids deserve to have teachers who dream wildly for them.

GIVE THANKS

After someone has spent time sharing with your students, be sure you are showing your most sincere gratitude. Handwrite a thank you note and mail it to them. Tag them on social media posts so that they can see how excited you are. Highlight the impact it made on your students (and you). Thank the dentist who sent your kids that box of toothbrushes. Thank that old friend from high school who sent your kids socks. Thank the rescue buddy who mailed your class new books from your Amazon wishlist. Not only does this express gratitude, but it may inspire other folks to give back to the kids in their neighborhood schools.

DON'T BE AFRAID OF A NO

It's wonderful that so many of us are eager to provide support to kids and families, and that we have opportunities to connect with other change agents in the community to walk with on our journey. Don't ever feel like you need to do everything alone. Engage your community. There are more good people out there than bad. Folks are waiting in the wings to give back. Take a risk, ask the question, and don't be afraid of getting a "No." Our kids and families deserve to have connected teachers.

MOVING BEYOND VIA REFLECTION & ACTION

Share out your reflections & action steps on Twitter using #MovingBeyondEdu

REFLECT:

- In what ways have you partnered with the community outside of the school walls? Consider houses of faith, businesses, local government, social service agencies, etc.

ACT:

- Form a team of like-minded allies (this may include your building leadership and/or social workers) and together, curate a collection of local agencies and the services they provide. Include a list of hours, addresses, phone numbers, and how to find them on social media. Present this curation to your building staff. Remind staff of this curation during larger events that have a lot of parents coming through (e.g., Curriculum Nights, Parent-Teacher conferences, etc.).
- Find a new place within your community to volunteer and meet people. Identify times in the year that may be more conducive to volunteering. Identify your passions and find an organization that matches your passion or interest!
- Go on your social media accounts and identify

different agencies and organizations. Start Following! Build your community network by supporting different agencies' special events (either by engaging with their posts (sharing, liking, commenting, etc.), promoting or attending the event, or sharing information with those you serve.

- Create a Community Calendar for fall break, winter break, spring break, and summer break. Highlight free or low-cost events that families can participate in. Include agencies' information and what services there are.

BEYOND YOUR TEAM

BUILDING YOUR NETWORK

I have this weird thing that happens to me over and over again, and I'm starting to get a complex about it. Have you ever had a Teacher Bestie? That one person in your building that you connect with that you can giggle with, swap stories, share supplies, or safely vent to on those bad days? I've had a few over the years.

But they all move.

Seriously, they all pack up and move. Not just to another school district, but other *states*. Do you see why I'm getting a complex? Chrissy Davis and Jeanette Simenson, I'm looking at you ladies.

Anyway, there have been years where I have had a Teacher Bestie and other years where I haven't. During those years when I don't, I always get a little tinge of jealousy when I see folks who have their Teacher Bestie, but I know that change is a constant of life, and I know more Teacher Besties will come into my life over the coming years.

Regardless of our T-B status, we are always working with the other adults. Many times, we're not only working with them, but we serve the other adults we work with—we are specialists that can provide support!

We talk constantly about collaboration. It's almost become one of those staff-meeting-Bingo-game-words. (Don't lie, you know you've played it before: one of those buzz words that comes up so frequently you can accrue credits, or at least draw an X on your common words/phrases boards to help get you through your next 60-minute staff meeting).

And to be honest, we are *constantly* collaborating. We rarely work alone. As advocates for our multilingual learners, we know that we need allies in every corner, and we need seats at every table. We serve on IEP teams for our students, we serve as team representatives for building leadership teams, we are on grade-level teams and multilingual education teams. We try to secure a spot on district-level teams to ensure that our students are in mind when making decisions. We support our classroom teachers in their understanding of scaffolds matched to proficiency levels. We collaborate with parents that we serve so that they are supported. We are never alone...

... But wow, is this a lonely job sometimes.

As we seek to serve and lead and flip lenses... we are constantly surrounded by other people. However, it is easy to feel like an island.

I know this is not a feeling reserved for EL, Bilingual, and Dual Language teachers and leaders. I know that many folks in many content areas have also shared this very sentiment, but I can only speak to it based on my experience and from my lens.

As an EL teacher, sometimes you are excluded from grade-level meetings, or even celebrations meant to show appreciation for all teachers. As a Bilingual classroom teacher, you may feel unable to relate to the monolingual classrooms, or feel that you cannot collaborate on shared lessons as much as you'd like due to a restrictive language allocation plan. As a Dual Language classroom teacher, you may feel excluded by the rest of the grade level team because you may be the only or two outside of the monolingual grade-level classrooms. You may be working feverishly towards a biliteracy model while the rest of the team is working on literacy in one language… and that can feel lonely if you don't have a team that fully understands multiliteracy. Sometimes you may be seen by others as self-isolated.

Typically, there are only a handful of EL specialists (which includes our bilingual or dual language educators) in each school building. It is so easy for us to feel like an island. It is so easy for us to take on the advocacy role full throttle, but it is also quite easy for us to be burned out quicker. Think about it: as the school year starts, the EL specialists are gathering and updating state paperwork, screening dozens of new students, starting their state paperwork, meeting with teachers, trying to schedule EL services, etc. By the time October rolls around, we are already exhausted!

I'm hopeful that as you read this, you will shake your head saying that this is not the case for you. I'm crossing my fingers for you. However, after talking with folks in the field across many states and school districts, it is my hunch that you may feel lonely, too.

We must have allies in our settings, and we do need to invest in our relationships with our colleagues. Even more, we need to trust our teammates and our teammates need to trust us. If you're allowed, keep "teacher chocolate" in your classroom and invite others in when they need a little something sweet. Keep a stash of greeting cards in your desk drawer, and drop them in your colleagues' mailboxes for birthdays, special occasions, or just randomly. Send a quick email thanking a teammate for a thoughtful comment during yesterday's meeting that pushed your thinking. Thank a colleague when they do something kind for you or your kids. Build a positive culture on your teams and in your buildings. Practice random acts of kindness. Leave change in the vending machine and put out a plate of cookies in the lounge now and then. Hold staff meetings in classrooms instead of common areas so you can get inside others' classrooms. My favorite professional learning comes when I can walk around in other people's classrooms!. Invite your colleagues to fun happenings with your students. Actively pull them in and lift them up. Those relationships are important.

I have been blessed by teammates and colleagues over the years. Deb Poehmann, a 4th-grade classroom teacher, once dropped off boxes full of Valentine cards for students to choose from (like the cool ones with wrestlers and temporary tattoos). Paula Smeltekop, our school librarian and now 5th-grade teacher, dropped off a bouquet on my desk to boost my mood. Melissa Evans, our gifted/enrichment teacher, popped in to help me prepare class gifts and wrapped over half of the presents for me during her plan period. Teammates have handed me tissues while I cried or left an encouraging note in my mailbox. Those are the moments that have brought me comfort, joy, relief, and an immense bubbling over of gratitude. We all need to receive those moments and we all need to give those moments.

There have been moments during staff meetings where someone goes in for that hard question before I even had to go there. Someone else asks the question that I always ask. Someone else steps in and pushes that issue that you were going to push. When this happens, we need to call it out and thank our allies, our friends, our teammates. Let them know that it meant something to your students, your families, and you. It matters. Let them know that you saw it, you heard it, and you appreciate it. We have to acknowledge that work! It may be because you have sparked a change in the tide. It could be something that has genuinely been on their hearts for a while, but this is the first time they've said it out loud. It could be because they've heard other people start to voice their concerns. It could just be where they are in their journey. Regardless, we need to acknowledge it, appreciate it, and celebrate it. Those moments are worthy of our attention.

...But, yes. You may feel that there are folks that you are working closely with who still don't "get it." They still may not understand why you fight so hard. They don't understand all the extra steps that you are taking to ensure that students have access, opportunity, or a voice. They don't know the overwhelming sense of fatigue and frustration that takes over when you have to raise your hand in a staff meeting (for the 417th time that same school year) to ask if the school letter will be translated into your top languages.

This is a hard space to be in, as a lonely voice in a crowd of many. If you are lonely in your fight, I see you. And the truth is, we all see you.

This is why we need each other. We get it. We hear you. We know what you're experiencing. We have been in those same shoes over and over again.

But how do we find each other? How do we build each other up so that on the bad days, we can turn to the ones who get it?

Don't throw stuff at me, but honestly... you have to go online.

It gets worse... Social media transformed my practice. I know, I know. I'm sorry. But I'm not sorry. I'm thankful because I am connected to hundreds (thousands) of teammates who have been there, done that, and bought the t-shirt.

These teammates are on every platform out there: Facebook, Instagram, Twitter, Voxer, you name it!

For my self-care and self-management, I have utilized my social media platforms for different purposes. I have generally kept all of my professional networks on Twitter, my friends/family on Facebook, and my hobbies/interests on Instagram. However, there are days and times and seasons where they all mix and it feels good to me.

I have found so many educators on my Twitter feed that keeps me going. They inspire me on the days when my internal fires are barely a flicker. They teach me so much, and I feel like a better educator after their posts pose questions that push my thinking. When I get stuck, they point me to resources, suggestions, tools, and ideas. I have bonded with folks who live across the world. Some have even become my Facebook friends, where we now have gotten to know each other personally. I have Twitter friends that will now wish my son a happy birthday and will giggle with me over the funny things my daughter says.

Through Twitter, I learn about professional development opportunities like webinars, conferences, podcasts. I can participate in as many (or as few) Twitter Chats as my heart desires. I can ask a question and I'm immediately connected to experts, gurus, researchers, teachers, leaders, and thought partners. My favorite researchers are a simple DM away. I'm a more informed educator, and I can connect those I serve in my district with the resources that I learn about on Twitter.

I am involved in online book clubs centered around multilingual education, like the amazing professional learning network (PLN) led by Dr. Katie Toppel (@Toppel_ELD), #MLLChat_Bk-Club. Each month they host an open book club around an EL-centered professional book or novels that are highly relevant to the multilingual learners we serve. It's great to be connected to other professionals in the field who I can learn from online.

I'll also go ahead and openly admit that I am a big FanGirl of other educators, and honestly I love that this is a thing now. There are rockstar educators that I follow online whose work resonates with me and inspires me. There are moments where I run into folks at conferences, and I have no problem being *that girl* who walks up to someone and says, "Oh my goodness, I follow you on Twitter! I love your work! Can we take a pic?" Yes, yes, yes. This is my style, and I'm not embarrassed; maybe I should be, but I'm not. Folks do this all the time to professional athletes, and perhaps I would too if I followed sports more and saw someone "famous" at Target, but I think it's great to admire other educators who inspire me to my best self as an educator.

Through Facebook groups, I have been able to connect with EL, bilingual, and dual-language teachers across the world. I can search for files that teachers have generously shared. I can search my groups for keywords/phrases on a topic I'd like to learn more about. I can ask questions when I have them, or post an encouraging message that I hope can help someone. I can ask for feedback from my peers on a specific piece of work I'm doing. When I want to find out how districts are handling something new, I have a full community to turn to that can share their experiences and expertise. I love groups like Advocating for ELs (run by Valentina Gonzalez), Leading ELLs (run by Pamela Broussard), and ESL Teachers K-12 (run by Margie Kirstein).

When I was a third-grade teacher, I used Instagram for teaching—a lot. I had a lot of visual inspiration from the images of other classrooms who were learning the same standards as my students. I knew I could reach out and ask questions of the educator on the other end of the post if I needed to, and it helped me feel less alone. As years went by, I realized I needed to dedicate one of my social media feeds just for fun (not work-related!), so my Instagram has become a place for puppy pictures, bright colors, and funny fashion bloggers I love.

It is important for us as we talk about self-care to track our moods and be intentional with how we use social media. It is easy to get swept up in mindless scrolling, but if you set limits on your time, and control your feed with who/what you're "following," that can help you with your intentionality. Check how you're feeling after you are online—are you stressed or feeling inadequate, or are you inspired? Be mindful of your social media interactions and who/what you follow.

It is critical that we stay inspired, empowered, and motivated. There's an old Spanish proverb that says, *Tell me who you hang out with and I'll tell you who you are.* There's another saying that says, *You are the company you keep.* Who we spend the most time with or associate the most is a reflection of who we are, and it's the same with our online interactions.

I will also add that it's really important that we diversify our online education feeds. If everyone we follow looks like us or had very similar upbringings as we had, I encourage you to broaden your perspectives by following others with different backgrounds, different upbringings, and different experiences.

By flooding our feeds with folks who have been in our shoes, it's easy to feel like you are connected to folks who care about fighting the same fights that you fight.

I wrote the following blog post out of appreciation for my online professional learning network (PLN):

From the Blog: When We Climb

Sometimes I look up and see the mountain standing before me, and I'm afraid it's too tall to climb. I gripe, complain, and I even blame all the people/systems/structures that made the mountain so tall. But I'm focusing on the wrong thing.

I look to my side and I see others. Some look beat-up. Others look fresh-faced, put together, energetic. Either way, they're ready to climb the mountain, too. They know it's going to be hard. They know they're going to fall a bit, get a little roughed up from time to time.

Some of the mountain climbers have tons of experience, or tons of privilege, or both. Some don't have any equipment with them and they have the wrong shoes on for this type of challenge. Some don't have any shoes on at all, but a fierceness is there in their eyes. They're still going after this.

I look down at myself. I feel ill-equipped. I feel defeated. I've tried to climb this mountain, and many others like it, before. I have some bruises, some scars, but there are still parts of me untouched and unscathed. I know my climbing days are not over.

I know that as I climb, as I push myself, I'll need to rest. I can do that. I can cheer on my fellow climbers as they push themselves forward, upward. When I'm ready, I can resume climbing.

When I fall, I'll know I can recover, and begin the climb again.

When I feel defeated, I may stop for a bit. I may need more time to recover from the uglier falls. The moments where I even question if I should still be pursuing this mountain. But that inward push will start again, and I'll know that I'm being called to climb this one.

When I start to give up, I'll pause. I know I can look to my fellow climbers. They're climbing up this same mountain with me. They're pushing for the same things. They're fighting tooth and nail, too. They give me the strength, motivation, and encouragement I need to keep going. In my dark hours I know I'll call out to them and they'll call back—still here too, and still climbing.

The mountains sometimes feel too tall. It may feel like there are too many. Sometimes we expect a tougher climb only to overcome them easier than we thought— knowing that there has been a foundation built at some point, by some other climber. Their faces have moved on but their impact has touched this space.

The hills we climb give us confidence. The mountains we tackle give us humility. The fellow climbers encourage us. We remain hopeful, optimistic, and dedicated to each mountain. We are educators.

We look to our left and our right and see that we are not alone—there are many of us. You can pan out further and see dozens, hundreds, thousands, and even more still are climbing this mountain with you.

You have a support system—a team—a family. All are ready to fight the fight along with you. They may be climbing for a thousand different reasons, but all are ready to tackle it.

We can climb the mountains ahead of us. We'll need each other and we'll cry out to each other. We'll share the tools, the tips, the ideas, the words, the space, the platform when we need it—*and we'll all need it.*

Here's to my fellow mountain climbers. Upward, my friends!

When we are in the business of advocacy for our students, families, and communities, many days it does feel as if we are trying to climb a mountain. It's overwhelming. This is why we need to have a team. If the folks in your school or district aren't climbing the mountains with you, look outward. Ask for help, go online, build your PLN, and get the support you deserve. This is too tough a journey to walk alone.

MOVING BEYOND VIA REFLECTION & ACTION

Share out your reflections & action steps on Twitter using #MovingBeyondEdu

REFLECT:

- How are you building your relationships with staff in your building? How do you show support for them?
- How are you using your social media platforms to build your professional learning network?

ACTION:

- Identify those who are in your corner. Who do you trust in your school building? How can you nurture and build trust with others?

Folks on my team that I can turn to:	Folks in my school that I can turn to:	Folks in my professional learning network I can turn to:
1. 2. 3.	1. 2. 3.	1. 2. 3.
Ways I can nurture the above relationships and build trust & community?	Ways I can nurture the above relationships and build trust & community?	Ways I can nurture the above relationships and build trust & community?

BEYOND TODAY

HOLDING ON TO HOPE

*D*ear friends, this work is not easy. We all have days when we come home and cry. We all have those moments where we have started to draft resignation letters. In this field, we face opposition. Sometimes it's not even from the opponents we expect, but from teammates who may mean well but do not understand the philosophy, or from administrators who don't have experience serving multilingual learners, or from a community member who doesn't respect or value linguistic diversity.

People are going to get mad at you. A lot. You're going to have folks that you thought were allies turn against you, roll their eyes at you, and try to run your name through the dirt. Let them. Disrupting spaces of privilege is hard for many people, and they may not get it. They may get it in five years, in fifteen years, or not at all. Your job is to keep pushing.

Familiarize yourself with the community, the school, the district. Have conversations with the veteran teachers. Have conversations with the newer staff. Understand where they've been. Acknowledge the growth.

When you know a difficult conversation is coming up, practice saying it out loud. Write down some of the exact phrases you'll need. Memorize them. Record audio messages on your phone or video messages on your computer. Be direct and firm, and speak with confidence. Know the counter-arguments and be prepared. Familiarize yourself with the myths about biliteracy and multilingualism and be ready to debunk them with research and facts.

Don't send emails when you're angry. Write it all out somewhere else, but not in an email. Come back to it with fresh eyes later. Vent at home.

When you find problems, seek out solutions. Identify possible action steps. Don't expect to solve problems overnight.

Stay brave when you feel like caving. Don't be afraid to acknowledge it when you're using your voice, "This feels uncomfortable to say/ask, but I'd like to push myself to say it: Have we considered…?" This may inspire others to use their voices, too—and that is quite powerful.

Celebrate your students and do it often. Celebrate with your families. Color pictures together, play outside when it starts to get nice out. Let them ground and re-ground you.

Keep up your A-game. Research constantly. Read a ton, ask questions at conferences and workshops, and make connections with folks in the field. Seek out experts, but remember your own experience and expertise as well. You will be asked to provide facts. People won't believe you and will want data and spreadsheets and pie charts, and you've got to have them at a moment's notice to back up what you say at that table where you fought so hard to be. Keep a file of all your favorite graphics that support your points in the most meaningful way.

People will call you out when you're wrong, and that's okay. I'm wrong a lot. While it's not easy to be called out, we have to grow from it and do better. We can't know it all, all the time. Be humble, reflect, and grow. Take criticism with stride. Take care of yourself, grow yourself, and get back to the work a little wiser each time. Reflect in whatever ways you need to: vlog, blog, meditate, pray. You have to grow to know.

Teaching for equity and change is a delicate dance where we take baby steps (and some days/meetings/events—they're more like GIANT LEAPS) forward every day. Sometimes when steps are taken backward (or even to the side), it feels like an earthquake. It feels like you're not making the progress you thought you were making. It feels disheartening and frustrating. You'll be ready to throw your hands up. You may have to take a few of those steps to the side (or even backward) within the same week. But note, during seasons of change, there are hills and valleys. There are highs and lows. There are days we move forward and days where no movement is felt. When you think you "failed," fear not. You didn't—you pushed someone's thinking, you asked the tough question, you advocated for a need, you used your voice to amplify the voice of others. That, my friends, is a success.

There is no small win in education. Every win is a big win. Every step forward is *a step forward*. Pause. Breathe it in. Feel the small change, acknowledge it, celebrate it, document it. Note when a colleague asks the questions that you would normally ask. That's a win. Note when a translation is done for families without even asking. That's a win. Note when a teammate tells you they want to help. That's a win. Note when a colleague asks a really good question. That's a win. Note when folks have conversations about linguistic oppression. That's a win. Note when a colleague asks to visit your classroom. That's a win. Note when a colleague invites you into their classroom. That's a win. Note when you're invited to join the committee. That's a win. Note when the district invests in an inclusive service delivery model. That's a win.

There is a natural progression in moving systems forward.

YOU are shifting an entire school community! Embrace the cha-cha, embrace the dance, and celebrate all the baby steps and giant leaps forward! I'm proud of you and I will always have your back!

Stay inspired, seek out help, and stay the course. Your kids deserve it. Your families deserve it. Your communities deserve it.

You deserve it, too.

And if all else fails, please take these words from the brilliant minds of our future leaders, because we all believe in you, too:

I believe in myself. I can do hard things. I can work really hard. I keep going when things get tough. I can get help when I need it. My teachers believe in me. They love me and care about me. I am important. I am loved. I will do amazing things!

ACKNOWLEDGMENTS

To my husband Eric: You are my world, and I cannot thank you enough for your relentless support and love. You've carried me through so many difficult moments, always taking the time to provide encouragement, space, endless patience, and empowerment. Thank you for always understanding my passion to do what I do, and for holding my hand through it all. Thank you for coaching dodgeball teams with me, for building my students a stage, for attending all the events, hauling all the pumpkins, fixing all the borders I couldn't reach on my bulletin boards, and so much more. I am so lucky to be your wife.

TJ and Chloe: I am so blessed to be your mama and I love you way more than I can possibly express. Thank you for cheering me on. Always look out for each other and for others. TJ, always keep your strong moral compass. Chloe, keep leading with your inclusive and empathetic heart. I will always love you both beyond words, no matter what. We will always be your safe landing. Also, Honu is so cute.

My sisters, Ashley & Danielle: My two best friends in the universe. Thank you for always being my biggest cheerleaders in life. The Nemeth Sisters are my safest place to be my truest self. You two are where I draw strength. You are my lifeline!

My mom and dad- Joy & Jerry: You two have done so much for us and for all of our babies. You are incredible parents and legendary grandparents. Thanks for believing in me so much and inspiring me constantly. Your strength, love, and unwavering support has always kept me going. I love you, and I am endlessly proud to be your daughter.

My friends: Karina Paul, Christina Cooper, Zully Zamora, Amy Ziemann, Chrissy Davis, Jeanette Simenson, Katya Naymen Chen, my cousin Taylor Oritz- I love you all and I'm so thankful for you ladies!

To All my Teammates, Past & Present: Thank you for helping me to grow. I am better because I've learned from you. Keep fighting, keep advocating, REST, then fight some more. I'll always have your back, and I'll always be your teammate.

My PLN: Special thanks to my Teach Better Family & the TB Ambassadors- you inspire me and help me feel loved, connected, and supported. I cannot thank you enough for being such an uplifting community. You make me feel "home." To my EduMatch Family, Sarah Thomas, Mandy Froehlich, Melody McAllister- thank you for believing in me and supporting me in this journey! You've made this dream come true! Adam Welcome, Dave Schmittou, Traci Browder, Hans Appel, thank you for your invaluable feedback and constant inspiration!

To my friends & colleagues in the multilingual community- I'm thankful to learn from you every single day. Thank you for being such an empowering and supportive group!

To all the students & families I've had the privilege to serve: Thank you for teaching me about education, family, life, and what matters. A mis estudiantes: Yo siempre creeré en ti. You will do amazing things!

ABOUT THE AUTHOR

Carly Spina has 15 years of experience in Multilingual Education, including her service as an EL teacher, a third-grade bilingual class-room teacher, and an EL/Bilingual Instructional Coach. She is currently serving educators and leaders across the state of Illinois in her role as an Education Specialist for the Illinois Resource Center. Spina has engaged in the successful development of several parent outreach programs, tutoring programs, student mentoring programs, co-teaching initiatives, and more.

She is deeply passionate about equity and advocacy for multilin-gual learners and fights for access and inclusive opportunities for kids and families. She speaks at various conferences and events and has received several awards over the years, including the Illinois Education Association Reg Weaver Human & Civil Rights Award in 2015, and the Distinguished Service Award for Excellence in the

Team Category for EL Community Engagement in 2019. She was the WIDA Featured Educator in April 2019.

Spina is an active member of the multilingual education community on social media and enjoys networking and growing with teachers and leaders across the country. Carly lives in the Chicagoland area and is supported & encouraged by her husband Eric and her two kids, TJ and Chloe, and quirky rescue pup Honu Pua.

EduMatch

PUBLISHING

Made in the USA
Las Vegas, NV
13 December 2024